Praise for Amanda Boyden and *I Got the Dog*

In the wake of a betrayal by the love of her life, Boyden must find the strength to rebuild a life in ruins. I Got the Dog is a luminous memoir written in stunning prose about the power of perspective and the reclamation of self-love. By turns, joyous and gutting, this is a book that begs to be read and reread.

—Maurice Carlos Ruffin, author of *We Cast a Shadow*

Amanda Boyden's *I Got the Dog* is a curious, fascinating memoir, at times magical, at times mystical, and always rendered in vibrant, seductive prose. Life has a way of offering unexpected turns of fate, some of them entirely unwelcome, and Boyden doesn't shrink from her own jolts and tremors. In the end, though, with humor, compassion, and raw honesty, she leads us to a place of beauty and redemption.

—Dinty W. Moore, author of *The Accidental Buddhist*

This searingly honest memoir is a rare thing, offering brilliant writing and integrity without compromising entertainment value: I was held from the first page. I Got the Dog is about love, hope and human resilience—a book for our times.

—Kate Kerrigan, author *Ellis Island*

A memoir of survival, bold and gorgeous in its telling—I Got the Dog fearlessly excavates the towering figures of Amanda Boyden's past and the shadows they cast, while allowing the writer to step into the light and reclaim a brilliance all her own.

—Sonja Livingston, author of *Ghostbread*

Amanda Boyden's *I Got the Dog* is a thrilling ride with one of the most original writers working today. Boyden navigates through our current crazy COVID-19 infected world without ever losing her humanity and grace, and flashes back to the floods of Hurricane Katrina. While death, illness, freak accidents, and heartbreak all occur, we sense she is the ultimate survivor, and can help us persevere as well. I loved her kindness to her parents and, of course Fry, the dog of the title. Every sentence sparks with original synapses. I think she's a genius!

—Laura Shaine Cunningham, author of *Sleeping Arrangements* and *A Place in the Country*

Amanda Boyden's memoir is astonishing. Boyden pulls off a full-blown literary miracle with the chapter "Then. With Notes.". Her most painful memory is expressed in a ground-breaking style that sets two recollections of it side-by-side, revealing how a brutal assault can resonate to this day. Boyden also traces the implosion of her marriage to a Canadian literary superstar and winner of the Giller Prize. These are merely two threads in an even-handed, marvelously detailed, and deeply-felt story we all recognize— and recognize in ourselves. We bend. We mend. We Rise.

—Honor Molloy, author of *Smarty Girl: Dublin Savage*

In *I Got The Dog* Amanda Boyden tackles the unwieldy suitcase of her life, unpacks it bruise by bruise, with such a deft hand, that you will be startled to realize how much of it you are carrying with you as you close the last page of this wonderful book.

—Colin Broderick, author of *Orangutan*, editor of *The Writing Irish of New York*

In the end what I found most remarkable is this memoir's generosity in regard to every person who appears in its pages. Never dismissive, the narrator is deeply attentive to each of the figures who come and go from her life. In the end, the world she observes so closely opens to a life of wonderment and joy.

—Kathleen Hill, author of *She Read to Us in the Late Afternoons: A Life in Novel*s

Amanda Boyden, ninja warrior, dares others to read *I Got the Dog* and hear her say, "I want to love you, and I want you to love me back. Here I am, vulnerable, naked, writing. I am not afraid to tell my story and lay myself bare to the world." And I say, bravo. Boyden gives other women permission to open up and tell their own stories, to unleash themselves, in the pursuit of their own freedom from the bondage of secrecy. This is a life-changing book. I know, because it has changed mine.

—Louise Post, singer-songwriter producer

for *Pretty Little Dirty*

"Glorious, modern, satirical and funny... Utterly realistic, compelling, artfully done, and also relevant... A first novel of complex truth and beauty."

San Francisco Chronicle

"Gripping... A brutally real reminder of the awesome power, and responsibility, of being a best friend."

Life Magazine

"The novel builds up a rhythm so hypnotic and alluring that to stop reading is a struggle... Boyden marvelously captures the wonder, terror and excitement of first experiences."

Philadelphia Weekly

for *Babylon Rolling*

"A brilliant, nuanced portrait of pre-Katrina New Orleans."

The Times-Picayune

"Few contemporary novels are, at their root, as compelling about the relationship between a city and the people who live there."

The Globe and Mail (Toronto)

"*Babylon Rolling* takes place during the year leading up to Katrina, ending just before the devastation starts. The reader knows what's coming, even if Boyden's sprawling cast of characters does not, adding an underlying sense of dramatic irony to the novel."

The Toronto Star

"Explores the fissures of class and race on a street where America's diversity is writ small... She orchestrates the voices of her characters like a composer, well attuned to the varieties of human speech."

Chicago Tribune

"The five story lines build into a terrifically vivid portrait of a city and its people."

San Francisco Chronicle

Amanda Boyden

I Got the Dog

A Memoir of Rising

Lavender Ink
New Orleans

I Got the Dog
Amanda Boyden

Copyright © 2020 by Lavender Ink, an imprint of Diálogos Books
All rights reserved. No part of this work may be reproduced in any
form without the expressed written permission of Diálogos Books,
except for short quotations used in reviews or essays.

Printed in the U.S.A.
First Printing
10 9 8 7 6 5 4 3 2 1   20 21 22 23 24 25

Book design: Bill Lavender
Cover Design: Daria Milas

Library of Congress Control Number: 2020939786
Boyden, Amanda
I Got the Dog / Amanda Boyden;
p. cm.
ISBN: 978-1-944884-81-9 (pbk.)
          978-1-944884-83-3 (cloth)
          978-1-944884-84-0 (ebook)

Lavender Ink
New Orleans
lavenderink.org

I Got the Dog

For all our lost dragons

*I do know how to pay attention, how to fall down
into the grass, how to kneel in the grass...
Tell me, what else should I have done?*

Mary Oliver

Prologue

COVID-19 isolation, 2020, New Orleans. Easter Sunday. Today, here, the holiday sounds like wind in old live oak trees and gunshots down the street. The sky has been gray all day and it's wicked hot. They say a storm is on its way. I have been quarantined in my apartment for nearly two months now.

Before dark I take my dog Fry out back of my building. I hear party noise from the third story. A man I know a little, somebody who used to be a pro athlete, leans into his wide-open window, his ass on the sill. He is naked from the waist up. He has people over. I can't tell how many but spy at least three. We're not supposed to do that, I think, as I traipse around after Fry.

The ex-athlete is nice enough as a neighbor though. There are over forty of us in the building. Every time I let out Fry, I have to touch multiple hallway fire doors and exterior and interior doors to reach outside and get back in. I try to follow wise cultures who've not had easy access to running water for centuries. I have a dirty hand and a clean hand for the task of getting my dog outside to use the small patches of grass in between the parking spaces.

Some of my very best friends live only a few blocks away, but I can't visit them today, can't sit at their long table on their back screen porch and take off my mask, eat with others, dip my feet in the respite of their pool. Instead I'm making myself a giant pot of soup for Easter. Without ham. I've never liked ham. My pot of soup could feed a dozen people, but it's just me. Another day of just me. I'll freeze the rest of it, save it for later till I move out of this place at the end of June when my lease is up. I wonder if I'll still be wearing a mask then. I call my father, states away, and we exchange food preservation small talk. Don't refrigerate potatoes, I tell him. My apartment fills with the scent of barley and thyme.

I miss Jazz Fest and the wafting weed smoke in the crowds, line-ups for crawfish remoulade, bumping into friends. I miss singing alongside strangers, smashed together, shoulder to shoulder. To live on the precipice of a completely new world makes me look back at the one that's gone and wonder, after this storm, whatever will our Land of Oz be?

Eight or nine years into my marriage. Post 9-11 New Orleans. Joseph went for a bike ride along the top of the levee, the highest ground in the city. I don't know what he contemplated on those rides. He pedaled out into the thin winter sunlight and made his heart beat faster. I rollerbladed the same path on other days, daydreaming about the future.

My writing nook in the one-bedroom apartment was carved out of a hallway. I sat with my back to the front door and tried to construct sentences on a computer screen. Behind me, I could hear Joseph return with his good bike, clomping it up the front stairs with less than his usual care. He rang the doorbell even though he had his key. I opened the door.

A lump. He had something in his arms. His wadded hoodie.

"I stopped," he said.

Of course he would. Somewhere. He always did.

Still in the doorway, bike propped on the porch rail, he revealed a crow wrapped in his sweatshirt. He'd found it on the levee dragging a wing, unable to fly, likely hit by a car.

"Bring it in," I told him, what he knew I would say. We named the crow Virgil. We nursed him for a time. We loved the wild, damaged thing, so much us.

The Before Now

My sister Meg, at two years and ten months old, fell off a curb and cracked her skull on the pavement of a busy Chicago street.

Mom watched the fall from a hospital room window many stories up. She'd just given birth to our youngest sister Emily. Dad wasn't allowed to bring Meg or me in to see her or baby Emily. We had children germs. So Dad hatched the waving plan. We could wave to Mom and Emily to our hearts' content. Only problem was, Mom's room was super high in the building, and we couldn't really see her or our new sister from the ground. No richy rich sprawling lawn at this urban Chicago hospital. Just a sidewalk and traffic behind us, the El clacking away in the background. So we stepped back, and then back some more, to try to get a decent view of our distant mouse-sized mom who smiled and waved as she held what looked like a blanketed peanut.

The way Mom tells it, the fall happened in slow motion. Dad, standing next to little tow-headed bird-limbed Meg, didn't see it at all. The way Dad tells it, Mom's horrified O-mouth and pointing finger clued him in a split second before Meg's icepick scream burst open the day.

───────

When I tell people that my sister Meg is a psychic-medium, their reactions usually fall into one of three categories: 1) feigned disbelief covering up the fear that Meg will know their biggest secrets in a heartbeat should they meet her; 2) complete enthusiasm and a desire for a reading; or 3) uncountable questions about how she "does it." How does Meg do what she does? How does she know those things?

I usually begin with the seminal story, The When I First Knew Meg Was Different Story. We three sisters are all three years apart, Meg the quintessential middle child in many ways. Some time during the summer that Emily was born—a few weeks or even months before the fall, although I can't say with perfect certainty—Meg, not yet three, started talking a lot. She talked nonstop. Insanely verbal, she chattered and chattered and followed me around till I went batty, Meg filling every waking moment with her voice. I usually wore my maroon and white vertical striped jeans and a random T. Meg tagged behind in floofy skirts or ruffled dresses, her stork legs and stork arms pale as could be, her fine white-blonde hair always in two peeps of pigtails. Mom used thin green grocery rubber bands with Meg, since all other hair ties slipped away.

Problem was, though, most adults couldn't understand her. Neither of our parents could understand her. But because of her constant presence in my life, I was the only person on earth that summer who could understand what Meg said. I could understand every single sentence. And she filled the day with them, the weeks with them. On and on and on she went. I begged Mom to let me play with my friends without Meg at my heel, but no such luck. Massively pregnant Mom mandated my first job, watching Meg when Mom wasn't. My eldest daughter duties were written in stone. Meg was my charge.

I wish I could say I was nice to Meg. I wasn't usually. Sometimes, forced by proximity and the usual sibling conflicts, I was cruel. Years later, I cut her Barbie's hair. Not so big a deal. But then I told her that there wasn't any Santa Claus when she was maybe six before I added that there wasn't any Easter Bunny and all the rest of the things, gnomes and Dumbo and leprechauns and Christmas elves and pots of gold at the end of rainbows, all of it, *all of it,* was made up by grown-ups.

Even worse, I ate the small piece of paper that contained the combination lock numbers to Meg's little pseudo bank safe, smaller than a breadbox, full of her strange treasures, and Meg couldn't open it ever again. She cried for hours, and I apologized to our parents after a spanking—despite their liberal bent, my parents hadn't read Dr. Spock yet—but I must have been really mad at Meg because I don't remember feeling regret even after my apology. (Ok, to be honest, we figured out how to open the safe later, since it was just a silly kids safe, but I'd seen somebody eat something secret on a piece of paper on TV, and I just *had* to eat that little combination note of Meg's. I also *had* to staple my finger once when a school friend accidentally stapled hers. "To know what it feels like," I told our mom when I came home from school with a Band-Aid and a note from my teacher.)

My pièce de résistance? I told Meg she was adopted (she is not) and she could tell she was adopted because she didn't look like Emily or me. Meg looked like a fairy. Emily and I looked like normal ragamuffins. I couldn't let it be though. I needed to add the clincher. I told Meg that she could go ask Mom and Dad and they would say, 'No. We gave birth to you.' That they would say 'Of course you're not adopted!' but that they were *lying.* Meg went crying to them and they said, of course, "No! You're not adopted. You came from the both of us!" A crescendo of tears followed. There was no convincing Meg she wasn't adopted. That time I felt shitty. Really shitty.

Still, miraculously, Meg never let go of her girl-child love for me, and these days I feel sick with loathing for the young Amanda. I don't know how I could have done most of what I inflicted on her. 'It's part of being sisters,' somebody might say, or 'You were just a kid.' Whatever. I was horrible to Meg.

But I did act as Meg's interpreter. Nobody else understood the perpetual stream of fledgling language that came pouring from her mouth every minute she was awake. Meg was hungry. She was always hungry with her hummingbird metabolism. She said she wanted more potato chips. Or more milk in her Lucky Charms.

Mom would ask, "What does she want?"

Dad would ask, "What did she say?"

And I'd reply, with a huff, "She says *she wants another peanut butter and jelly.*" I honestly couldn't figure out why nobody else understood her.

One summer afternoon when our mother was occupied, either watermelon pregnant or just after giving birth to Emily, Meg and I were doing something or other that kids did outside then. Maybe rode my bike around the block on the sidewalk with her little butt sitting on my back fender. Or picked our scabs and looked at clouds. Who knows. But we'd stopped whatever we'd been doing and stood in our driveway, waiting for the minute when Mom would call us inside for lunch. Meg wore a dress, of course. She despised pants. And this part, I'll remember all the rest of my days:

Meg, tiny little girl Meg with her skinny blonde pigtails in her frilly dress: "Before, I have a hat and blue flowers on it. My fave-it. And a blue dress."

Amanda, the ever-pragmatic tomboy: "You don't have a blue hat. You have hoods on your coats."

Meg: "Uh huh. A blue hat and flowers on it. Before. The blue dress is my fave-it. They together."

Amanda: "You're making things up. You don't have a blue hat with flowers. Shut up."

Meg, stomping foot: "Uh huh. 23 me, a blue dress made of godden and a hat flowers on it."

Amanda: "What is godden? You have white dresses and dresses with flowers. You don't have a blue dress and you don't have a hat with flowers on it. You're not 23. You're a little girl."

Meg, even more frustrated: "I a grow-up. In a godden dress. My fave-it."

Amanda: "You're not a grownup. You're a little girl."

Meg: "No now. Me, number 23 now."

Amanda: "Stop it."

Meg, pausing, desperate to figure out a way to communicate, finally: "Now. Now! Me me me me me my number now, my number twenty-three now. *Before*. Before now. My fave-it. The hat and dress, they blue. Godden."

Amanda, beginning to get an inkling of what her younger sister might be saying: "But you're a little girl. There isn't any *before* now."

Meg: "Yes, uh huh, yes! Before now. When I is I before me. My fave-it is the blue godden dress and the flowers on the blue hat. That! That! Yes! Me before me! Yes!"

———

Did Meg falling off the curb and slamming her head on the street cause her to say such things? Did it open up a portal to a place nearly all of the rest of us can't experience? Or did that head slam merely accelerate whatever otherworldly awareness

Meg already had? I can't say. I can't remember the order of things specifically to know with any certainty. I only know that Meg now has given over six hundred readings to people, largely strangers, and what she tells them makes sense to them in ways that stand up the hairs on their arms and makes their necks prickle. That makes them cry. They consult her about deaths. About murders. About atrocious things. But most of it isn't terrible. She nearly always offers a psychic salve that comforts. Meg has seen future wives and future husbands, people her clients have yet to encounter. She describes the clothes the future spouses will be wearing when they first meet, what they do for a living. Months or years later, slightly or a lot freaked out, the clients tell Meg that the initial encounter came about exactly the way Meg described.

Sometimes when she's giving a reading, Meg's hands seem to have a mind of their own. A few years ago Meg gave a reading to a grieving young woman in her late teens who'd recently lost her mother. Meg relayed what the passed mother wanted her daughter to know. Evidently the mother and daughter had a special sign language all their own. Meg's hands formed the sign as she gave the reading, and said, "She wants you to know this." Meg had no idea what the sign was. But the daughter did. It was their personal, unique symbol for *I love you*.

Past and future events and voices flow through Meg like seawater through a sieve. She catches enough to share with her listeners, and they carry home delicate shells, or a rare pearl, retrieved from the beyond.

———

At some point in her young childhood, Meg must have learned to stop talking about matters from the other place. She went through most of the normal paces, becoming a socially adept, if still sylph-like, popular girl in grade school. She made deep and abiding friendships. She wore Jack Purcells and bright red jeans or marigold yellow corduroys, makeup as soon as she could. She took to cigarettes early, maybe 11, playing Ms. Pac-Man at the laundromat and smoking with her friends.

Unlike other people, Meg never seemed troubled by troubling things when she was young. She cared for her boyfriend's Ukrainian grandmother for a summer job while the grandmother swore and swore at Meg in a language she didn't understand. Meg smiled and made the woman lunch, every day nodding, every day showing the grandmother once again where the bathroom was.

Meg went to the aid of a friend when the friend's brother committed suicide. In the family basement. After the police had left, as others mopped up blood and picked up teeth from the floor, Meg comforted her friend upstairs, assuring the girl that she was going to have a full life, and that her brother no longer hurt.

Meg excelled at art and didn't give a shit about much anything else in high school. So she decided to get her degree immediately and be done with it, at 16. She had to petition the school board to allow her to graduate early, though, and they insisted she test out of classes she had yet to take. How could she do that? The board thought they had her as a student for at least another year. Still, off Meg went to the room where they administered the written tests, never having studied any of the subjects. She says her hands filled in the dots, guided by more than her own volition. She tested out of all the classes.

She earned a brilliant ride to a great art college where she gained acclaim from her professors and fellow students alike.

The entities from the other place wouldn't let her be though. They knew Meg could feel them, hear them. They hung out on campus in the very old building that housed the Fiber Department looms, where Meg worked late into the night, a little human spider with her shuttle and dyed silk yarn. Sometimes, they poked Meg at house parties in dark corners.

Decades later, when Meg first decided to hone her skills as a psychic-medium, she focused on a local woman near her town who had gone missing in summer, sadly presumed dead. There was speculation that the woman could have drowned in a small local lake. The police had dredged the lake more than once, however, and had come up empty. Some weeks later, the missing woman's coworker talked to Meg and wanted to know Meg's impressions. Meg told the coworker that the missing woman was indeed in the lake. Meg said she was in some kind of a tube, underwater. Meg didn't know or understand what the tube was. But the missing woman had passed and no longer suffered. They would find her body in spring.

Officials recovered the woman's body. The following spring. She'd been in the intake water pipe of the very same dredged lake.

Over the ensuing years, Meg has sharpened her skills. She's learned how to make sense of what she's being shown, because that's how what she does works. She's being shown something, a visual scene, by a dead person to relate to a living person. Or if the passed person was a talker, really vocal, Meg's being told things. The people from beyond are using their preferred method of communication.

Often people want to know if their loved ones who've died are 'around' them, guarding or maybe just watching. Meg says that the deceased usually describe or show the living's surroundings to her as 'proof.' It's their point of view, of course. How better to let the living know?

A client asked Meg about her mother's presence.

Meg relayed that the woman sitting in front of her had a four-poster bed and that she hung clothes off one of the posts.

Yes.

That the woman sitting in front of her had a big dog that shed.

Yes.

That the woman's mother said her daughter needed to buy a hair-magnet hair-picker-upper thing and get the dog hair off her bed because that's where her mother sits.

The daughter shook her head in awe and laughed.

The woman's mother had forever pestered her daughter to get something to pick up the hair. It goes without saying that Meg had never been to the woman's home.

And so. "Yes," Meg told the woman sitting in front of her, "your mother is around, watching."

Another woman wanted to know the same thing about her passed mother: is she with me?

Meg related this:

You have a shower with a glass door. It steams up until it starts to drip. She's talking to you in the drips. She's writing words. I know it doesn't make any sense. But that's what she wants me to tell you.

The woman's mouth fell open. She didn't speak for a good while.

The woman and her young autistic son had recently started connecting with one another by reading what looked like words left on the glass door after a shower. Messages from Grandma.

In the summer of 2017, my still-then husband Joseph and I visited Meg and her husband Lance and their kids in Nebraska. They live on prized acreage in a beautiful part of the world, a tranquil and luxurious existence outside of Omaha. They rent their extra land to local farmers, and crops ripple away and down the gentle hills from their yard. Sometimes the farmers bring in cattle to eat leftover cobs of corn in autumn. Sometimes alfalfa perfumes the wind all summer. Coyotes call in the evenings from the copses of trees in the distance. Visual artists, Meg and Lance designed and built their own piece of heaven, and from their wraparound porch the chaotic pace of contemporary life can sometimes disappear.

Joseph swam with our nephew in the perfectly round pool as dovetailed swallows careened overhead. I couldn't keep off the oversized swing set, forever chasing a chance to fly of my own volition. Their large wooden picket-fenced garden appeared and receded with each pump of my legs on the swing. Tomatoes. Squash vines. The marked grave of their beloved brindle pit bull, Malcolm. Cucumbers, peppers, dragonflies, honey bees.

Joseph and I always loved being there, in summer especially. It seemed impossibly easy to carve out whole hours of peace. At least to me, we were happy, and happy together.

Joseph hadn't yet been completely decimated on social media, and we were preparing for an extraordinary meeting in Santa Fe a few days later. When we weren't outside playing, we were voraciously reading and brainstorming inside on a potential series based on a particular writer's life work—the secret possibility of a large project we couldn't tell many people about.

Two days before we were to fly out to Santa Fe, Meg cornered Joseph at the edge of the huge kitchen island that sits open to the large living room with its brazen and glorious prints and sculptures. Arguably the center of their home, the brown-black granite slab of the kitchen island anchors hearts and boots and so much more. Their current pit bull, a gentle white female who can actually blush pink on her belly, snored on one of the nearby sofas. Somebody from the beyond was clamoring for Meg's attention, somebody from Joseph's family.

Meg faced Joseph and glanced past him, or maybe completely through him. I stood next to him and then went to the stove to tend onions sautéing in olive oil.

"Who's having the baby?" Meg asked, glancing repeatedly over Joseph's shoulder, over his head. "Somebody is telling me there's a baby on the way. Frank?"

Joseph's brother, Frank, and his immediate siblings, all seven of them in their late 40s to late 50s, had finished having their families years ago, so a baby didn't make any sense.

Meg can sometimes relay information backwards, or just off of spot-on center. Understanding the dead isn't always easy. Loved ones who have passed can have trouble getting Meg to articulate specifically what they want to communicate. Sometimes they get grumpy with Meg. She tells them, 'Hey, I'm trying!' It's not easy when she's the only one watching their movies and listening to their directives.

Meg suggested to Joseph that he actually sit down in the next day or so with her in her reading space in the corner of the attached art studio before we flew out west. She wanted to give him something a little more purposeful and intentional. She pressed one more time, "Who—what about the baby?"

I missed Joseph's reaction. I wasn't looking at him, instead busy stirring the onions at the stove.

Later that night, Meg told me Joseph's face had gone sheet white.

For the rest of our visit, even though I pressed, and even though Meg pressed, Joseph wouldn't sit with Meg. He managed to avoid the suggested reading completely, barely able to look Meg in the eye for a normal conversation from then on.

Less than two months later in New Orleans, in the house Joseph and I had shared for a decade, in a city we had shared as a married couple for more than twice that, after a teary farewell to one of our dearest friends who was moving far away, after goodbye shots and protracted professions of love and dedications to stay in touch, after the friend left, long long after midnight, Joseph decided to choose that moment to tell me. He was expecting a baby with another woman. He was the one with the baby.

———

The rain began later that morning. It didn't rain for just an hour and then recede, the pumps doing their thing. It rained as if to destroy my neighborhood, to crush the city and everyone in it with waters from the sky. It rained to fill up the bowl that is New Orleans. It rained for hours. And hours. It rained to drown. It rained to wash away more than twenty years of marriage. I told my friend April in a crazed, freakish-sounding text, that it rained, it flooded, just for me. All for me, I told April.

Sometime around noon while the rains continued their battle to purge the city, my friend April appeared outside my door. She'd walked through rib-high waters to reach me. I opened the door and stared at her. Rainwater sloshed onto the hexagonal tile floor of my hallway. Water had filled the street and then breached the curb. It filled my planter beds outside and then made its way over the sidewalk and to the lip of my doors. I didn't care. I wanted it. I welcomed it.

I hadn't slept. And I'd sent Joseph away from the house to wherever he might find a place to lay his head.

April stepped inside. I'm sad to say that I didn't notice she needed a change of clothes until she asked me if she could have a towel and something dry to wear. She'd not been able to drive any closer to me than eight blocks away.

After Hurricane Katrina, I got into New Orleans quicker than most everyone else. Joseph and I had press passes (along with his brother and our friend Jarret) to report and write about the devastation. The floodwaters of a city are different than those in rural areas, but Louisiana is unique. Both the rural areas and the cities offer up unusual debris. Evacuating town after Katrina, we drove through devastated New Orleans East, heading towards Tennessee. The shoulders of the highway were littered with dead alligators.

Things float in the city: sometimes refrigerators and small cars, at least for a short while. And sometimes things disappear beneath the murky waters. In Louisiana, alligators can drown and later lie baking under the hot August sun after they've been deposited onto the higher ground of a paved freeway. Or alligators can actually continue swimming under the murky waters. In the city.

Used needles float. Or they don't. Submerged lawnmowers and motorcycles become invisible in the filthy swirl. Manhole covers burst away from the sewer holes they protect.

April, knowing the dangers, still trudged her way to me through the morass. I believe she understood that the worst thing in the entirety of my marriage had befallen me. I believe she knew I needed saving from the flood.

Systems were in place, in New Orleans, to save the city under such extreme circumstances, both during Katrina as well as the Saturday, August 5, 2017 flood. Outsiders might not understand the complications of our city: it is largely poor and largely swampy in its attitude towards everything. But it's also wise. It chooses to swing with the punches. It always says, *Laisse le bon temps rouler*. It tries and sometimes gives up. It says about humanity, 'Hey, we get it, get you, get almost everything even though we can't do fuck all about any of it.'

If you go screaming at the top of your lungs into an unknown row of modest houses in Mid-City, after having just witnessed a point-blank shooting to a man's head, the city will try to comfort you with a cool washcloth to your brow. Or to be more precise, strangers living in Mid-City will guard you close on their small front porch and try to keep you from further harm. This, I know, is true.

The 2017 August flood revealed plenty for New Orleans. It told us that the pump houses and the systems put in place to protect the residents of New Orleans weren't working very well yet again. An investigation determined that give or take half of the pumps in the city weren't functional at all. In 2017. Twelve long years after Katrina.

But that, now, for me and so many others, is water under the bridge.

———

My sister Meg and April know each other. Even though they have never met in person as I write, I suspect they consider themselves close.

I've known April for a very long time. Seven years ago, April's grandfather was murdered. I cried for her loss as she described her generous, curious, wonderful Pappaw. The circumstances of his murder were horrific. He lived alone. In the country.

I don't know how many years later it occurred to me to recommend to April that she talk to Meg about the case. The cops weren't making any progress and the trail seemed cold.

April contacted Meg, and Meg responded. Meg didn't ask any questions. She just wanted two emailed photos, one of April's grandfather, and one of April.

Like many of the others inhabiting the beyond who've reached out to Meg, April's grandpa tried to show Meg things. He tried to get her to step inside his skin and relive the moments he thought would show her what happened.

These are details being brought to new scrutiny. I can't share them here. The cold case is quite active again because April has kept it alive. Her pursuit of justice is unwavering for the memory of her grandfather.

Plenty of what Meg said to April made sense to my friend, to the point that she felt compelled to lie on the floor after she very first read Meg's written thoughts. Sometimes, God is in the details.

And sometimes, those who've passed choose the right details to deliver through a vessel like Meg.

Meg told April, "Your grandpa had a funny habit. He walked around the house and jingled change in his front pocket. He always did that."

A number of weeks after Meg had sent April her notes, a small group of us women friends that included at least one disbeliever gathered around April's kitchen island.

April stopped reading Meg's notes aloud. Her jaw hung open, certainly for what wasn't the first time after rereading Meg's feedback.

Meg had recently worked on another murder case with a father who'd lost his son in a grisly crime in the South. She'd gotten a location and street name, down to the description of a chain link fence—nothing that had ever been released to the public.

April stood and shook her head about Meg's words that she'd been reading. "It doesn't make any sense," April said. "None. *How could she know that?* Why would she know that? Pappaw did that all the time. He walked around and shook coins in his pocket, just like that." April demonstrated in some beautiful, odd body-memory way. She became Pappaw for a few seconds, and we all understood what Meg had tried to articulate. Meg had become Pappaw for as long as she could hold onto his tether.

The other women sat silent.

I did too. But I just felt proud of my sister. My little fairy sister Meg with the cracked noggin. I smiled a small smile as my eyes teared up. Bravo, sistah.

———

Systems were supposed to be in place to keep the bowl of New Orleans from filling up with water. Again. But half the pumps in 2017 were broken. Half the system failed.

Ultimately the metaphor hasn't been lost on me. But I have no other option than to move forward. I didn't choose for my marriage to break. I didn't ask for the floodwaters. But they came. Sink or float. Swim or drown. Sometimes the two options felt like they were one and the same.

Meg couldn't offer me much in the months after Joseph's revelation besides her loving sister support. But she knew I'd make it out the other end. She could see that much, but she could also see my tumultuous future journey. I don't bother her too often about the details. She doesn't have easy answers for me from The Before Now. And maybe that's best. Maybe it's enough for me to understand to my core that Meg, and the other who was Meg before, had a blue dress, and a blue hat, and that the hat had flowers on it. The outfit was her favorite.

My mother used to tell me it would hit me like a truck, the need for a baby. It never did. Before we married, Joseph and I talked about maybe or maybe not, ever, having kids. He was cool with that. He had a young son when we first started dating. Joseph told me he didn't need any more children.

I met the boy, still in diapers, when his mom brought him down from Toronto to New Orleans to visit. The sweet kid had just started on solid food but whined after the days of car confinement and didn't want to eat. Joseph's rental house kitchen had an Astroturf floor. I sat with the boy on the itchy plastic grass and made up stories with the steamed food on his plate. Look. The broccoli stalks were trees. What could the disks of carrots be? Rafts. We floated down the Mississippi on carrots, and the boy started eating. Several years later, Joseph's firstborn son had made imaginary friends. One of them was named Broccoli.

These days I understand something that didn't occur to me then. The son's mother, despite what Joseph told me, loved Joseph with her whole being. She thought the proof of that, the boy, could be enough to win him back to his country, to her, to them.

August 5, 2017, when Joseph told me he had gotten another woman pregnant, he asked me to raise the baby with him. He cried and said he knew of nobody else in this world who would be a better mother, a better influence on a child of his. I couldn't fathom the why of it. Or the how. How could he ask that?

Marrow

Dad lived for camping. Mom? She rode shotgun. She plodded along beside Dad two summers in a row in the early '70s with us three kids in tow. We didn't make small forays out into the natural world for a weekend, or even a whole week at a time. We took a long distance road trip for the *entire summer*, three consecutive months, two summers back-to-back. With just a tent, a Coleman stove, and a lantern.

Dad drove. The first camping summer, baby Emily sat on Mom's lap in the passenger seat. Through the entirety of the Southwest, both Mom and naked but diapered Emily sweat and turned a shade of rose, the same red-brown hair plastering their foreheads. The wind through the open windows never cooled us enough. Dad's left arm grew leathered and brown. Mom's right arm always looked angry. Meg and I draped ourselves dramatically across the backseat, both of us trying to catch a cool breeze that didn't materialize till weeks later when we'd reached Northern California.

I'd seen over thirty of the fifty states by the time I was eight years old, and probably a half dozen Canadian provinces. The strange gift of those traveling summer months has stayed with me, miserable as they seemed stuck in the back of an Opal station wagon for eight or more hours in a day. The Oregon coast still conjures crabs and fresh blueberry pie. The Redwoods feel like both home and a holy place, the grandest chapel I've ever been in. I stepped on glaciers. I trekked through Yellowstone. I fell head over heels for Mesa Verde. We collected shells in the Panhandle and wildflowers from the Oklahoma roadside. Dad's wanderlust fed our childhood. He studied and taught literature; he experienced countless rich landscapes in written variations. But his longing to see and touch other places in the physical world, that desire imprinted on the rest of us, a row of ducklings following the drake.

In that formative time for me, I believe Mom loved Dad. And maybe even more, she loved us girls. So much of what she did, she did for the women her daughters would become. On the marathon camping trips, Mom persevered. She hiked the Rockies with a child on her back, following in the footsteps of her husband, up the trail leading to somewhere. Possibly to just anywhere.

She cobbled together three meals a day from cans and roadside produce on a Coleman stove. She somehow disposed of her tampons and Emily's dirty diapers without drawing bears from the woods. She helped pitch the tent and roll and unroll sleeping bags. She did dishes with river water in a plastic tub, the same one she washed our dirty clothes in. She didn't complain. Mom, a voracious book reader, couldn't read while Dad drove. It made her carsick. She couldn't read by the light of the Coleman lamp at night either because we had to conserve fuel. I guess it hardly mattered. When she lay her head down at the end of the camping day, when I was supposed to be asleep already, I could hear her breath drop quickly into a regular rhythm. How tired she must have been each night, I can barely imagine.

When our family returned home to Chicago after months outdoors, we sisters were rarely content to be inside. We'd moved to a house in Oak Park, and when Emily cried and Mom couldn't soothe her, Mom made Meg and me bring her outside. Mom told us to sit Emily in the dirt. She calmed nearly immediately. We three sat in a tight circle beneath the juniper bushes in front of our house, breathing deeply. Meg and I showed Emily how to press her chubby baby palms flat into the soil surrounding us and leave prints. All three of us did, making a prehistoric rendition of a nest, palm print upon palm print fanning out from us till we'd surrounded ourselves in feathers.

I can venture a guess as to why our parents made the move, but it doesn't much matter. Money, likely. There were better opportunities to be had in St. Louis.

Sure, we were a Chicago family, used to free Shakespeare in the summer, visits to the Natural Science and Industry Museum, long evening chats with Dad's fellow PhD candidates. How could St. Louis be so terribly different?

Our parents opted to be near where our father's parents lived, only we couldn't afford our grandparents' neighborhood. Instead, we moved into a compound of townhouses in the suburb of South County populated by the likes of people we'd never encountered before. Missouri white people with strange accents piled on top of each other, squeezed in side-by-side, the Lincoln Log bunkers splaying out for horrible ill-planned puzzle piece-shaped block after block. The community pool teemed with kids, their sunburned and unwatching moms drinking their booze-filled sodee-pops. The curving edge of the pool, a monstrous misshapen kidney bean, was bordered with sharp red bricks. Because edging a community swimming pool with sharp bricks is an absolutely logical thing to do.

Our mom enjoyed the lakes of her Minnesota childhood and always swam as an adult, quite joyously, adept and graceful. She rescued me once from a hotel pool when I didn't yet know how to swim. I had the notion that I would walk through the shallow end of the pool water by myself till I could touch the floating buoy rope that demarcated the start of the deep end. Dad and Mom sat on lounge chairs, watching. I tiptoed, the water delicious, the independence even tastier. Till the bottom dropped out and under I went. Eyes open, I turned in circles, trying to walk back up the incline to the shallow end, when Mom executed a perfect lifeguard dive and swam towards me. I watched her in the gurgling underwater quiet, her arms and legs working, her face coming nearer, as my nose burned with chlorine. Mom saved me.

No shame on Dad, though. He knew Mom would be better at my rescue. Dad wasn't much of a swimmer ever. At 6'4", maybe 170 pounds, he had no body fat and couldn't even float. He made a point of showing us sometimes, how he couldn't float. He'd lie back in the water and down his legs would go, sinking sinking, and then his torso would follow, till finally he had to tread water to keep from going under.

At the South County townhouse internment camp that had become our new home, that dared to call itself a *Manor*, Mom never got in the pool. She was smarter than that. She never made any friends save for one woman who had moved into a unit that shared our backyard. The woman, brash and funny and about our mom's age, was from New York. Neither Mom nor she enjoyed where they were currently stuck but found a bit of pleasure observing and commenting on the new species around them, the strange caws and cackles, the lack of tribe civility.

Although the bathwater-warm water was tinged with pee, I loved the swimming pool. Kids and pee water, it's just not that big of a deal. I'd taught myself how to do summersaults underwater and gave myself the mission of accomplishing ten in a row without taking a breath before Labor Day. In and out of the pee water I went, launching myself up and out of the pool, stepping onto the hot concrete, visiting our mom, Meg trying to make friends, Emily splashing in the kiddie pool.

After weeks of my summersault practice, our mom's patience wearing thin for racist sunburned white people missing teeth, I propelled myself out of the community pool once more only to scrape my shin on the sharp brick edge. Ok, scrape is an understatement. Gouge. Gouge, or maybe chunk.

My leg hurt, but not so much immediately that I realized the extent of my injury till I looked down. I was missing a piece of my shinbone and the flesh that used to cover it.

Heading to Mom, weaving around the baby oil-slathered Missourians and their spawn sprawling in all their procreating glory, blood ran down my leg and over my foot. I left a trail of wet, red one-footed prints across the hot concrete.

I flopped down on my beach towel next to Mom.

"What did you do now?" Mom asked. (Yes, I regularly did things to myself, including swinging too high by my knees on the jungle gym and chipping off half my adult front tooth on the neighboring bar. While upside-down.)

"I don't know." I did know. I wanted to call out the stupid-ass brick edge on the pool but didn't know yet how to blame the system.

Mom blotted and stanched, other moms and kids wrinkling their noses, and then Mom and I both took a close look. "What *is* that, Mom?"

Mom pinched her mouth and looked away then quickly covered up my shin with my rumpled T shirt.

"No, what *is* that?" I repeated, pulling away the T. The divot wasn't bleeding profusely any more, but the scoop of where my bone used to be looked like a honeycomb in miniature. "Wow, cool," I said, bending forward to inspect further.

"Don't," Mom said. "Stop it." She glanced back at my leg, swallowing a gag. "It's called marrow. It's the inside of your bone." Mom had worked as a nurse's aide when young, and she always used proper terminology with us three. Boys had penises and girls had vaginas, not wangs or pee pees or 'down theres.'

I took another good look at my shin. Who knew that was in there, I thought.

The brick-lined community swimming pool wasn't what made our parents beeline us the hell out of South County though.

A late bloomer, I crushed easily on boys but had nothing to physically show them. Sometimes I won them over with my tomboy I-can-do-anything-you-can-do bravado, but not too often. In the nexus of Bigot Nirvana, directly across the way from our building, I'd set my sights on a boy I will call Mark T. He was short, no taller than I was, which couldn't have been more than 4'8", with a head of wild wavy hair down to his chin. Who knows the whims of girls. But this guy did it for me. I was 10 years old.

Mark played with me. I decided to show him that I could carry a bamboo cane and jump rope at the same time. I fell and skinned my knee badly. I still have the scar. His mom yelled at him, cigarette dangling off her lower lip, to get the fuck inside. A few days later, he explained in one enlightening afternoon that sometimes his dick—I didn't know the word, had never heard it before, so he grabbed his crotch for me—yes, his *dick* was sometimes hard and his sister let him sit on her and sometimes it went inside his sister. He and I were the same age, his sister a young teen.

Thinking that was the strangest thing I'd yet to hear, I went straight back to our parents and told them at dinner. "And he said sometimes he sits on his sister and his dick goes inside her."

No doubt our parents were absolutely horrified, watching Meg to discern how much she was taking in. After asking me what other new words I had learned and I spouted off many more than they had anticipated, many culled from Mark T.'s mom with Mark T. explaining their meaning, Mom and Dad tactfully shut down the conversation. I couldn't figure out why, but I was no longer allowed to play with Mark T. of the Manor after that.

Surely finances had something to do with our parents holding firm in South County, even after the Mark T. sex ed lesson. A good girl, I listened to my parents, so they needn't have worried I'd disobey and let Mark T. sit on me.

Instead, I took up with a girl named Lonnie a few doors down. She was an only child living with her single mother. Her mother had a beehive at least eight inches tall, sprayed to perfection, quite the anomaly in the mid '70s. Lonnie turned me onto make-believe crushes on famous people you couldn't touch or talk to. I didn't get it but played along. Covered in posters, her bedroom retreat fascinated me. Her mom allowed Lonnie, just nine years old, to subscribe to teen magazines, many of which came with an inserted Shaun Cassidy, Donny Osmond, or Leif Garret. Lonnie always had a new crush. She'd kiss the posters provocatively. I was fascinated. Home to dinner I went.

"Lonnie says kissing with your tongue is how you do it," I told my parents. "Like this." I stood and walked to Meg sitting in her dining chair and grabbed both her cheeks in my hands, going in with my tongue extended.

"Amanda Elizabeth!" my mother screamed.

The next day Mom and I visited Lonnie and her mom. Mom said it was just to see that Lonnie's mom was as nice as I said she was.

Lonnie's mom was super weird and way older than our mom, with a completely amazing way of decorating their townhouse. Her favorite colors were red, black, and gold. She had covered the entire living-dining area in black and red flocked velvet wallpaper with gold accents. Her giant lamps had towering gold shades edged with fringe. She never opened the heavy drapery, and her gold velvet sofas were covered in protective plastic, something I'd never in my life seen before. Lonnie's mom wore thick black eyeliner and skinny black pants and chain-smoked.

Lonnie and I headed up to her bedroom while Mom and Lonnie's mom made some semblance of polite conversation.

Fifteen minutes later, I had to leave.

At dinner, Mom told Dad that Lonnie and her mother lived in a bordello.

I asked what a bordello was. They didn't answer me.

"What's a bordello?" Meg asked.

Dad, working his ass off at a new job, seemed less concerned about Lonnie's mom's décor. Mom tried to express that it was the iceberg tip to a much bigger problem that was the whole of the Manor way of life. But our parents were forever tactful around us girls.

The next day I went to Lonnie's and told her that my mom said that Lonnie and her mom lived in a bordello.

Yeah, so it was just Meg-n-me, going it alone after that. We'd walk to K-Mart on our own for fun, through the back alleys of industrial courts, stopping at an empty playground that served some other sprawling ass-backwards community to swing on the giant swing set. We carried our hard earned allowance money and bought small potted plants, sometimes a slinky or live swimming goldfish. We'd become something akin to friends at that point, seeing as how neither of us had anyone else to play with in South County.

One late afternoon, Meg and I found ourselves at the Manor, sitting in the empty planter bed that topped the creosote railroad tie retaining wall abutting our 'desirable' end row unit. We were ten feet off the ground, planting seeds from K-Mart packets. The bed always presented itself there, dusty and bare, and we thought we'd put in flowers.

Our heads down, we chattered about how pretty the flowers would be and how we'd pick them and put them in vases in our rooms and all around the house.

"Hey," somebody said.

An older boy, a teen who I recognized as one of Mark T.'s sister's friends, stood down below, looking up at us in our dirt-filled ledge perch. His lanky blond hair hung over one eye. He had his hands in his pockets. "What are you doing?"

"Ignore him," I told Meg, and so we did, willing him to leave us alone while our digging became more self-conscious.

"Hey."

Nothing. Us? We're just digging here. Go away, I willed.

"Hey."

"Hey."

Meg was the first to look.

At the dinner table that night, Meg spilled the beans. "A boy showed us his penis today," Meg said. "It was pink and long. He wiggled it."

Forks down. Knives down. Mom gave Dad the glance: I told you so.

"What?" Dad asked.

"Nothing," I said.

"What happened?" Mom asked.

"Nothing," I said. To be honest, I told Meg not to look and that we needed to leave, which we did, crawling back down, Meg's undies peeking out beneath her dress, before we headed up the stairs to our place with the perpetually unlocked door.

"Uh huh, yes," Meg said. "A boy—a *teen*-ager—showed us his penis. He stood and took it out of his zipper and went like this." Meg gestured a flaccid waggle, but I'm not sure her motion did anything to help the situation.

I tried to play it off. No biggie. But our parents wouldn't have it. I copped to having seen the kid before but that I didn't know where he lived in the internment camp. They extracted from me that Mark T. and his family knew the kid.

The police came. They talked to Mark T. and then found the kid, talked to the teen, and let him go. As a relatively innocent girl, I couldn't figure out why it had become such a big deal. But it had, and the neighbors started in double-time on the gossip about the trespassing Chicago family.

We began house hunting the next weekend, with the blessing and financial help of Dad's parents. And voilà. The entirely opposite, privileged suburb of Clayton spread itself in front of us like a smorgasbord of cultural and educational opportunity.

———

Mom and Dad eventually split when I was a high school sophomore. The timing sucked for me, but I'm sure it sucked for our parents even more. They'd tried to make a go of it. They got counseling. It didn't stick. Mom had started working nights in food and beverage. Dad still worked days. They were no longer the people they used to be.

After the divorce, Mom took us girls for a vacation up to Minnesota, the land of her youth and where, at that time, the entirety of her extended family still lived. She came from great stock. Mom was a Viking. Well, she was a former ice skating princess of Germanic lineage, and she needed some support.

To help keep her awake over the slow-going miles between St. Louis and rural Minnesota, Mom wanted us to sing out loud with her. Her favorite song had long been—or quite possibly the only song she knew all the lyrics to—Helen Reddy's "I Am Woman."

We daughters knew all the lyrics too.

"*I am woman, hear me roar,*" Mom sang.

We didn't even groan. We had the song in our bones. Mom had been singing it for years. "*In numbers too big to ignore!*" we replied.

"*And I know too much to go back and pretend.*" Mom's voice cracked. Riding shotgun, I could see she was crying. She glanced back at Meg and Emily in the rearview mirror.

"*Yes, I am wise, but it's wisdom born of pain, Yes, I paid the price, but look how much I've gained. If I have to, I can do anything...*"

We sang to fields of wheat. We sang to an early moon in the blue sky. We sang to each other in our little cruddy car crammed with girly things and tomboy things and Mom's remains of the day. But on and on she went, another mile and then another, down the road. She'd get her daughters to where she wanted them to go, one way or another. Someday we three would be invincible because the lyrics, and Mom, made us believe it could be so.

In the last year, our mother was diagnosed with early stage memory loss. Seems there are so many permutations of age-related dementia these days that they group them all under one umbrella, the most understandable or recognizable being Alzheimer's. So Mom's got it. Mom, the lifeguard whose talents saved me as a kid. Mom, who moved us the hell out of South County. Mom, who hiked mountains with a daughter on her back.

Dad faces his own gauntlet. We in the immediate family have all grown close again after the 35+ years since Dad and Mom divorced. Mary Anne, Dad's wife, is in the late stages of Alzheimer's, six years after diagnosis, and against the advisement of professionals, Dad continues to be Mary Anne's sole caregiver. His days fill with repetition and routine. They no longer go out to eat at restaurants. They no longer have meaningful conversations.

Mom asks Emily and her family and Dad and Mary Anne to come to her small bungalow in St. Louis for holiday meals. They never turn down the invitation. Mom has always been a great cook and baker, and she can still host and take pleasure in the occasions. She sends Christmas cookies home with Dad and grandkids alike, studs a ham with cloves for Easter. Watching Mary Anne at the table with newfound attention, Mom quietly processes the notion of memory loss and then carries on. She plans for and relishes each meal with family. She is aware of time.

Medication will extend the memory years that Mom has left, but there's no cure yet. None of us sisters are witches—although we've been called that on occasion—but oh how we would love to cast a spell and stall Mom out exactly where she is now. This past year Mom passed her mandated driving test. She baked strawberry shortcakes for Emily's birthday. She takes out recycling and weeds her backyard flower garden.

But we daughters, too, are aware of time. In the interim between now and the next step, we will try to divide the weight, the burden of slow sorrow. We will try to relish some of the natural world still and again with Mom, maybe take her back to places she'd remember. Yellowstone or the Pacific coast of Oregon. Maybe just the beautiful Nebraska view from Meg's wraparound porch, the scent of everything growing green hitching a ride on a breeze, tomato blossoms, knee-high corn, so much alfalfa. Someplace peaceful where we can tell Mom it'll be ok no matter what.

These days I stare at my spread fingers in downward dog or arm balance and think about the passage of time, recall those hours we spent as girls under the front yard juniper bushes in our feathered dirt nest. Tattoos cover my forearms now, my recording of years. My hands show age. But they hold my weight. Pressed into the earth, they ground me still. I set my intentions before my practice of making shapes with my body and will myself to stay brave, to be kind, will myself to be as good to our mother as she was to us. We can do this, I tell myself. We can do this, I repeat.

When not in his campus office, my father graded his students' handwritten bluebook essays in our Chicago dining room, grumbling. I wasn't allowed on those afternoons to practice my gymnastics in the adjacent living room, which bummed me out. He should be out at the college, I thought, although to this day, the musty book scent of academic halls inspires in me a combination of aspiration, entrapment, and dread.

Joseph recommitted himself to teaching before I did. We'd had a rough ride in grad school as TAs, sometimes teaching two-thirds of a full professor's load for a pittance, and it had left a bad taste in my mouth. I'd rather hang upside-down over the heads of strangers.

A few years into his stint as a fulltime instructor, Joseph had ingratiated himself fully with faculty and students alike. He is a charming individual. I first encountered the young woman, the student, in Joseph's office. While I stood there, the snaggle-toothed snot strutted in a literal circle around my husband as though she owned him. I suppose she did.

The student followed Joseph and me to our summer teaching-abroad gig in Spain. Afterwards she, the lemming to the end, along with her friends, followed Joseph and me to Rome for our post-teaching getaway. Back in New Orleans, she sent emails under a false name to me, telling me my husband was having an affair. Finally, when he'd quit her, she left a copy of his book under my car's wiper blade, Joseph's inscription to her still there, his dedication page to me torn out.

In Lieu of a Career

Ask kids what they want to be when they grow up, and all the parents at the backyard barbeque will lean in. Keisha wants to be a doctor. Zoe wants to be a lawyer. Alejandro's going to be a web designer. Jeremiah is going to open an animal shelter. Some mid-range options that don't freak out adults too badly: chiropractor, baseball coach, grocery store owner. Then the slope gets a little slipperier: race car driver, manicurist, cocktail waitress at a casino, professional football player. Sexy dancer. A Kardashian assistant. Somebody who invents new gum flavors. A social media influencer because then she doesn't need to go to college and can just make *tons* of money and drop out of high school and shop all day and try on clothes and take selfies.

My parents asked me for years, and I never came up with anything. "You don't want to be a teacher?" Dad asked.

"What about a chef?" Mom suggested, projecting a bit because in the day the back-of-the-house food and beverage industry was dominated by males.

No matter what they suggested, I wouldn't have it. Until one day, while working on my ninja skills in the kitchen, trying to kip up from the floor and getting in the way, I knew exactly what I wanted to be. "I'm going to grow up and be a cat burglar."

"Well," Mom said and paused, looking at Dad who pulled a crisped fatty bit off the resting pork roast. I watched Mom hold her tongue. "So...what would your duties be as a cat burglar?"

"Stealing jewels. And climbing walls." I did a backbend.

If the jobs had actually been invented at the time, I might have chosen a paragliding instructor or a Cirque du Soleil choreographer.

"You know stealing is wrong," Dad reminded. "A cat burglar is a criminal, you know."

"Not really," I said.

Dad frowned but his eyes wandered back to the roast. "What would you do with your jewels?"

Mom looked on.

I shrugged then came up with something. "I'd sell them." I shimmied my way up the kitchen doorjamb and spoke from above their heads. "They're not criminals. Cat burglars just take things from rich people and sell them to other rich people." Like Robin Hood, I intimated, only not quite as good.

The first job I had that earned me actual money was in construction, when I was seven. I built a 'haunted' tunnel out of cardboard moving boxes. I coated the inside of each box with repulsive household substances among other things to turn the tunnel into a sightless sensory overload experience. Vaseline, a sandy sea of white sugar, grass clippings, a long swath of soupy mud. I hung Tang-soaked rags from the ceiling and put the contraption on the front sidewalk. Towel flaps kept my clients from seeing too much of the interior. I charged three cents per crawl-through, two for a nickel. The neighborhood kids showed up in droves. I raked it in. After the kids returned home covered in crap, their clothes ruined, I was banned from crafting a haunted tunnel ever again.

C'est la vie. I had grander employment aspirations. In high school, the need for money got real. I needed new Vans and a better skateboard, track cleats. Since before our family's move to St. Louis, Mom had worked in food and beverage, and she hooked up with a cool restaurant she eventually came to manage, a classic. It had connections to both sports figures and vaguely, uh, Italian families.

The restaurant sported multiple valets, a salaried piano player at a baby grand five nights a week who modeled himself after Liberace, and—gloriously lucky for me—a coat check room. Miss Christine, the very elderly aunt of one of the Italian investors, was given the coat check room's income in perpetuity through a will. Or something like that. But Miss Christine, also a hostess, doddering back and forth in her formal long velvet black skirt, couldn't be both a hostess and helm the coat check room. And money proved better when a dressed-up young woman accepted the full-length minks and the cashmere coats handed her way. Mid-October weekends onward, I was Miss Christine's gal. She split the tips with me 50/50. Seemed fair to me.

When sometimes a quiet few minutes arrived, I'd walk through the rows and pet the foxes or lay my cheek on a sheared beaver. The whorls of curly lamb looked like clouds. Sandalwood cologne, Chanel No. 5, the room smelled like money. Checking coats in the days of disco excess equaled solid, easy income.

Science, specifically medicine, rocks. Gimme anything corporeal in nature and I'm fixated, utterly. So no big surprise that my work-study jobs in my first year and a half at Wash U involved the Science Department despite the fact that I was a comparative arts major. I spoke Spanish in intensive language workshops, danced my heart out in modern dance class, studied literature, and then I headed to The Row.

The Row consisted of an underground bunker of windowless rooms all branching off a single long hallway. Located in one of the many science buildings on campus, it had a keypad entry, high security for the times. Each room contained different animals. I fed and watered the rabbits, monstrously huge brown beasts that were part of what I could only guess was a study on metabolism. I changed the cedar shaving bedding of countless mice containers, including some that weren't white and kept in a separate part of the room. I asked my boss what the brown and black and gray mice were for, and why they were separated. Those, he said, were fed to the rattlesnakes. The snakes didn't like the taste of white mice. But one of the grad students working with them speculated that the white mice had been so long bred from the same genetic background that they didn't behave like mice of different colors.

I learned that baby mice reach a growth stage called popcorn mice. They jump like popcorn popping, and they proved impossible for me to catch and transfer into a clean container. My sister Meg, still in high school, came to The Row a few times to help with the endless mice tubs. The popcorn mice always boinged out of their small cages and onto the floor, scrambling under rows and rows of wire racks and into corners. Meg squealed and laughed as we both crawled on our bellies, reaching for the barely haired pinkies.

I fulfilled some of my student-worker hours on the weekends, all alone. Nobody else ever came into The Row on those creepy Saturdays and Sundays, the entire building feeling abandoned, post apocalyptic in its silence save for the penned creatures doing their thing, the gigantic rabbits changing their positions in their cages, the mice—those lucky enough to be given more space—running on their squeaky wheels.

One weekend I coded myself in on the touchpad and entered the concrete center hall to have a vampire bat dive bomb me. The vampire bats were kept at the far end for a study on blood coagulation. Or that's what I'd invented in my head. Why else would vampire bats make good science subjects? As the only other living being in the long hallway, I equaled food to the bat. Some irresponsible, chicken shit grad student had let the bat out and hadn't bothered to recapture it. Or, yeah, that's what I'd invented in my head. But I didn't have a key to the secondary lock on the bat room. I couldn't help return the thing to its home. I only knew to go about my duties, ducking and waving my arms as I zigzagged from mice to rabbits, rabbits to reptiles, working my way down the hall as the blood-honing bat squeaked and flew in echo-location ovals up and down the corridor, trying to alight on me with each loop.

I escaped the hallway eventually, although I suspect the vampire bat never did. It was gone by my next shift on Monday afternoon. Occasionally, though, I daydreamed about the bat in class. I stared out the window and wondered if it had gotten free. If it did, could it actually crossbreed with a regular bat? Would it find love with a norm? Would it resort to feeding off squirrels? Secretly, I rooted for the vampire bat.

I never waivered as a reliable student-worker employee until my duties expanded. After some months on The Row, I was asked to take on the feeding of the rattlesnakes.

The juvenile gray and black and brown mice had grown on me. They let me pet them and I let them crawl on me. They seemed to appreciate my presence in their lives. The mothers were good to their young. How could I be responsible for their deaths?

A freshman's decision-making skills aren't particularly honed. Or at least mine weren't. I decided to 'rescue' two of my favorite mice, a black one and a brown one. I stole a container, bedding, and food and smuggled them out late one night. The end of the semester had arrived, as had my release from my uncomfortable roommate situation in the dorms, so the mice came home with me to my family bedroom. And the house's other pets.

The mice lasted less than a month before the cat figured out how to open the cage. Neither the cat, nor the mice, escaped their destinies. I cried.

I took time off of college for no reason other than that I was straight-up burnt-out from studying and happened upon a killer opportunity. When I was 20, I travelled to France because I was supposed to model. I'd been a finalist in a contest and caught the eye of a top agency.

It didn't go well. I have an abnormally large ribcage and nothing fit. I was a terrible clothes hanger, and my attitude didn't help. I asked too many questions, drawn moth-to-flame to the other side of the camera. I wanted to see and do what they did. And the *all* of Paris fascinated me far more than my brainless job. To this day, I hold close the nearly palpable memory of the grooves in the winding stone steps of Notre Dame leading up and down the towers, put there by centuries upon centuries of footsteps.

Post Paris, I started at the Kansas City Art Institute—KCAI. My 6 AM clock-in time for my breakfast waitressing shifts on Saturdays and Sundays hurt. My sister Meg and I worked at the same diner, and on weekend nights we usually stayed up till 2 or 3. I'd quit cocaine at that point. For a short while I'd dealt drugs, occasionally to famous people. My cover was driving the stretch limo of a boutique hotel. The other women chauffeurs and I wore fitted tailed tuxedos and relished our brushes with fame. Because I'd been a dealer, I had access to all the coke I'd wanted. Professional athletes and celebrities alike loved the stuff. It had a very tame reputation. Then. Me, though? I liked it too much. With a modicum of self-awareness at 20 years old, I stopped cold turkey. So mornings were rough without chemical assistance after almost no sleep. But the line cooks dished up delicious pepper and onion-laced hash browns, eggs and eggs and eggs. We learned to carry six or even seven plates at a time. Coffee coffee coffee. We bought our groceries with piles of coins, our drinks at clubs with quarters or single dollar bills.

About the same time, I responded to some interesting job ads and word-of-mouth leads. Starving art students might well be even hungrier than starving artists.

An old man who placed an ad for an assistant ceramic tile installer really just wanted company. For months he paid me just to have lunch with him. We never grouted a single tile.

A professional photographer needed a nude model. I knew a classmate who'd landed the gig before me. Why not? I was majoring in photography, the other side of the camera. But hey, I could get paid to stand as an object again.

The photographer went after very 'real' photos. A number of times, while I stood in front of a white paper background, he asked me repeatedly to drop my left shoulder. 'Farther, drop it farther,' he coaxed.

Only after I'd seen the black and white proofs did I understand what he'd been after. He'd wanted my breasts to appear as uneven, as lopsided as possible.

Another session, he asked me to draw something on the big white backdrop in charcoal. I drew giant sharp-toothed monsters because I felt like it. And I thought that he'd expect me to draw flowers. Immediately after I drew my monsters, I did a naked front walkover. At his request, I did more walkovers, again and again. From the proofs some weeks later, I knew what he'd been after: the noticeable dimple in my ass cheek that appeared only in the moment when my leading leg nearly touched the ground.

Then I agreed to pose for something I didn't want to do.

Photographer dude liked to take close-ups of the female anatomy, and even though I felt funny, I let him.

Later I saw the proofs.

Why did he do that?

Why did I do that?

It was a job. My face wasn't even close to the photographic object. You'd never ever have known that it was me.

In retrospect, I likely did it for two reasons. One, the money. Money, maybe especially in undergrad, is valuable currency. To feed oneself. To go see music on occasion…pay bills. Meg and I didn't have much coming in from our parents. And that was fine. Neither of us blames them for what they couldn't have possibly provided at the time, but it did make us creative in our money-making endeavors. I certainly went far beyond what Meg ever considered. She never crossed a line.

Two, the attention—not from the photographer but from a couple of fellow students, guys I had my eye on, guys who respected daring women unafraid of their own bodies or of showing it in photos. Attention, it's a ravenous pull. Years ago, when my then 'tween niece started taking selfies, I couldn't believe the trend: true self-objectification. Now I can barely imagine a world without selfies. I take them. Sometimes I go for weeks without one; sometimes I take several in a single day. Because, hey, you can never take just one. Recently I got stir-crazy during a hurricane that didn't materialize, waiting for the power to go out, the same continuous cycle of weather people saying the same things. I donned a short purple lace negligee and matching knee-high purple rubber boots: my pretend traipsing-through-flood-waters ensemble. I stood in my hallway and took photos in the big round mirror then texted them to somebody whose attention I wanted. Look at me! Desire me! Tell me that I have a nice ass. Then look me in the eyes and say I'm smart.

One autumn and early winter I worked as a house gutter cleaner in the North Shore suburbs of Chicago. My brother-in-law Lance was kind enough to help me make a living while my musician-boyfriend toured. Lance's wife, my sister Meg, was attending the Chicago Art Institute for her teaching degree, and I'd make the journey down from Milwaukee for a couple weeks at a time to climb huge extension ladders in freezing weather and hand-scoop dead leaf gunk out of rooftop gutters with Lance.

He and I had the nifty notion that if we eliminated the safety task of tying ourselves off to either chimneys or each other working opposite sides of a roof, we could save enough time on each house to actually squeeze in one additional job per day. We were paid by the house, of course, no matter how big or how sloped the roofs, how icy the slate, how perilous the task. Once I stood on Lance's shoulders, while he stood on a ladder, on the pitched rooftop of a massive house, three stories up, in order to try to reach a short stretch of gutter spanning a fourth floor attic dormer. I suppose we were hungry for money. That, and the small start-up company we worked for encouraged customer feedback and inspection.

Choosing to not tie off, we came up with the next best thing, something we decided was pure genius—unless we actually needed to use it.

So you could gutter clean one of two ways back then. Bring a bag up to the roofline with you and fill it with rotting leaf gunk as you slowly moved down the length of the gutters, climbing and descending the ladders every four feet or so, picking up the ladder and moving it forward. Or you could actually sit on the roof itself and pitch the crap from up top and onto the frozen ground below and rake it up when you got down. Moving the massive ladders that were necessary to reach the North Shore mansions' rooftops was no easy feat. So we opted nearly always for the method of flinging the putrid decay by the fistfuls onto the ground below.

It's possible we were too poor to be sane:

Climb up the monstrous extension ladder. Then climb up and over the top rung and the lip of the gutter and onto the rooftop. Hope it's not icy. Turn around 180 degrees, and sit down. Look over the edge of the roof to see how far you'd fall. Look down the length of the gutter to see how clogged it is. Lean over and start scooping. Toss. Scootch your ass to the left or right a few feet. Scoop and toss some more. Keep going.

We considered ourselves lucky if owners had planted any kind of evergreen bushes close to the house. We didn't need to rake gunk out of them, just jiggle it into the bushes instead. Like mulch.

We had some near accidents. But hey, our improvised safety measure would have worked. Maybe.

Sit cross-legged on the very edge of the rooftop looking over and down. Ignore your fingers turning into icicles inside your thick rubber gardening gloves. Assess the risk of falling. If great, do the thing. Stick one foot fully into the cleaned gutter at that awkward angle. Go on. Sandwich it in there like a work boot sausage inside a tight bun. And keep going. The gutter will likely tear away from the house. And the leg will likely break in multiple places. But if you fall, you will probably not smash onto the frozen ground. You will dangle by your broken leg from above till help arrives.

We considered it a decent safety measure.

———

When Joseph and I moved to Toronto after graduate school at the University of New Orleans, I happened upon a path I'd never considered previously. He and I rented a space in a cluster of converted warehouses on the near west side. Living in a new country, I didn't quite know the lay of the land or what to do with myself. Out my window one day, I saw a woman about my age tending to her building's communal garden. I introduced myself and learned her name was Nisha. I asked if she knew of a place with a trampoline. I wanted to exercise but grew bored of treadmills and gyms. Rather than guide me to a trampoline, she invited me over to her loft space a few days later.

It was the first day of the rest of my trapeze life.

Decades earlier, when I was seven or eight, Mom and Dad watched Olga Korbut, the famous gymnast, performing in the Olympics on their little black and white television. Because of the time difference, my parents actually woke me up late at night to watch this wonder child-woman perform. I was groggy, Mom and Dad awestruck. They had discovered how to get me out of their way in the kitchen and let me constructively burn up energy. I have Olga to thank for the ensuing years of gymnastics lessons and then team practices and then state meets and then nationals. Gymnastics? Next best thing to cat burglar ever.

By the time my trapeze days started, I relied nearly solely on muscle memory. I'd never, ever considered running away to join the circus, but a new lust for all things aerial bowled me over. Single trapeze—the non-swinging kind. Double trapeze. Triple trapeze. Flying trapeze. Silks. Hoop. Anything up there, with or without a net, sang their siren songs to me. To bolster my resume, I made sure to refresh a few ground skills too. Contortion, tumbling, hand balancing.

After a year and half away, Joseph and I moved back to New Orleans. It, too, has a siren song. When a friend begged me to teach her trapeze, we found a warehouse space in New Orleans. We enlisted a few other so-inclined women, rigged, and started training. Eventually we started performing. I helped found the New Orleans School of Circus Arts (sadly now defunct.)

I started teaching freshman composition at about the same time. I'd perform several stories up in the air, no net or safety lines, in front of hundreds or sometimes thousands of people on a Saturday night and grade essays the following Sunday afternoon. Diverse skill sets. I just barely eked out a living.

After juggling both for years, I had a sludgy, unclear, niggling realization. I could do neither much longer at full capacity. My true love, what I'd been born to do, had tugged at me for so long. And I'd almost gotten there. Almost.

In the first years after graduate school—I attended the University of New Orleans Creative Writing Workshop, specializing in fiction—I embarked on a novel. About a down-and-out circus troupe touring through the Deep South. I finished it. I was proud of it. I landed a New York agent. And she put the book up at auction. We were to hear back from the editors and their publishing houses quickly. On a Friday. On September 14th. In 2001.

9/11, a Tuesday, ate my first novel. Not a single editor bit, and why would they? New York, and the country, no longer cared about anything other than what was at hand. The publishing world pulled many, many novels slated for release. I was hardly the only writer affected. But I mourned my own personal, small loss, even as I trained trapeze with my troupe for an upcoming gig. That next week, one callous or maybe clueless troupe-mate I'd recruited from yoga, (of all disciplines!) said that she ultimately didn't care about the towers, about what happened in New York, that we should quit talking about it and move on. Because, hey, her life wasn't really impacted in any way she could determine.

Some months later, after repeated tries at selling *The Art of Hanging*, I listened to Joseph who said I needed to write something new or I would shrivel and die a slow writing death. He was right. I started *Pretty Little Dirty*. I gave it all I had. Because I'd decided that I never wanted a What If when looking back on my life.

Writing a book-length work is a blind, solitary endeavor full of doubt and the chastising voices of creatures that sit in opposition on your shoulders. It is a thankless job. It is ambitious. It is crazy. It is so often fruitless. But I doggedly trudged on. And I decided that if I were to be 80 years old and still sentient, I could only do one of the two jobs I most loved, trapeze artist or writer.

I passed the trapeze baton to my most skilled and senior troupe-mate and put all my eggs into the writing basket.

———

Some of my other stints: makeup artist for music videos, freelance illustrator, go-go dancer, bartender, interior house painter, bit-part actress, caterer, housemaid, proofreader, tutor, painter's nude model, cafeteria server, stunt woman, human statue, New Orleans reveler-for-hire.

A funny thing about jobs. You can put your heart and soul into them, make them your life, or you can leave them when you walk out the literal or figurative door and go home for the day. Most people sorta straddle the divide.

With the exception of trapeze and writing, I don't know that I've ever put my whole heart and soul into my work. It's possibly the reason why I've had so many jobs. When investment is minimal, the pain of changing course or leaving is minimal. And change can feel invigorating. Change can feel like progress. Just the notion of *new* can feel like progress.

Decades ago, I spent some time flitting through different crowds. Doing so seemed like a mind-opening, kinda cool thing. At one point I hung out with a very mixed group that included two women working in the sex trade industry. That's not what they called their work, not back then. They weren't high-end escorts. They weren't selling *The Girlfriend Experience*. They simply said they were whores. No, they weren't strippers, definitely not dancers. Yes, real life whores, they assured me. They sold themselves for money. They very vocally emphasized the fact that they were independent. No pimp, not ever.

I didn't know many other whores well, just those two, but I hung out with them for a couple of weeks when they were finished working for the evening, or afternoon, whatever they decided for that day.

The two of them and I, along with the rest of the motley crew, maybe eight of us, partied, got wickedly drunk one night, and somehow the confessions began. These two women who had professed earlier in the week to feeling empowered by their choice to sell themselves, feeling like they were their own bosses and doing what they did because they liked it, well, they both began describing their freaky experiences with the johns. The storytelling started in the comedic realm. Then they moved to the belittling experiences. Then the humiliating experiences. Then the violent experiences. Both young women cracked open like broken suitcases. They were not proud. They were not empowered. They hated their jobs. They cried.

Last I'd heard, maybe a month after quitting that crowd, both women were still at work selling themselves for money.

To what limits would you go for money? I don't mean that Demi Moore movie where Robert Redford pays her a million dollars to sleep with him. I mean, would you try to cross a border illegally if it meant feeding your family? If your only options were illegal, would you still do what you could to protect and provide for your loved ones?

What about the jobs that don't pay well considering what is involved? Would you race into the burning towers as a firefighter, in New York or in Paris? Or would you, as the hired guard, crouch in a hallway and not respond during a school shooting? What if you were that same scared school guard and you were a single father and your two daughters would be waiting for you at the dinner table that evening? And you never arrived.

Who are the people attracted to the out-there weird jobs? Who wants to grow up to be a Brazilian waxer? How about a morgue make up artist? Maybe a sadistic bent draws you to body piercing. Maybe a fetish makes you want to kneel on the floor in front of a woman and slip her foot into a perfect, tiny size six and a half stiletto.

I used to think, having put myself through years of graduate school that, much like the mandatory conscription in Norway's military, everyone in America should be made to do a solid six months of service in the food and beverage industry when they turned 20. Nope, no frat parties for you this next semester. Gotta bus people's uneaten food. Gotta go bend to take an order and realize the patron is talking into her Airpods instead of to you. Listen to every specialized request with a smile, knowing you'll have to argue with the kitchen to actually make it happen. Refill countless iced teas. Endure the disrespect. Endure the tedium and visible waste. Endure the people expecting to be *served*. Get stiffed for tips. Learn what it's like to see the other side of the table. Learn what it's like to be treated like a peon, sometimes as the most lowly, subservient human with whom your customers regularly interact.

Even so, there are invisible gradations everywhere in the service industry. We just don't usually see beyond the person who comes to the table.

I worked at the cheese counter and coffee bar of an international grocery and dine-in café/hipster place ahead of its time in St. Louis when I was in my late 20s. The owner, a liberal Jewish man whose family had endured plenty, decided to sponsor an Eastern European family that spoke no English and who'd never lived outside their village but were under persecution in their homeland. The newly arrived husband became the restaurant's dishwasher.

My boyfriend at the time and I, along with Meg who helped me land the job in the first place, became so close with the dishwasher that he and his wife invited us to dinner at his family's new home, a tiny bungalow in Dogtown. They had a son, maybe five, who smiled and had already learned some of his new land's tongue. The kid was a wonderful translator. The dishwasher and his wife served us a feast of traditional dishes. Most were so foreign to our palates that they confused us. A yogurt course? So much meat. Course after course, they offered us their country's signature dishes, the cornucopia on cherished decorative china overwhelming.

The yogurt was house made and the meat the most gracious display of generosity that the family could afford. I worried that the dishwasher had spent half his paycheck on the feast.

The dishwasher? He wanted to be able to work out on the floor someday. He aspired to waiting tables. He took English lessons every week. He wanted his young son to have an American life and to have his son choose whatever job he could possibly imagine. The dishwasher learned the word "astronaut," and at work when he could catch my eye as I dropped off tub upon tub of dirty dishes, he said the word carefully and whistled then smiled, gesturing, sending his dripping hand and arm up into the air, pointing at the sky.

The worst job I ever had was one that likely many people would gush over. It was relatively recent. The job necessitated that I write much of the work that Joseph was to be given sole credit for. We worked on a prospective television series that never got filmed. In other words, it's all actually moot. But from the development of the "bible"—the rules for a series—the invention of the fictional town, the characters and their traits and voices, the setting, the intricate themes and the plot twists, through each and every episode of a full series, all the way to completed scripts, I wrote and wrote. I threw myself into the task.

I wasn't the only one who did so. But we others were invisible. The credit was to go to my ex, and that was that.

Why, at the end of the day, couldn't I let that diss go? Why couldn't I reconcile the fact that I was part of a "team" of writers, only I'd never get credit for my skills, my time, my effort, my heart, my intellect? *My words*?

I guess because I wrote my heart out. Again and again. But my name would never have appeared on screen as a writer.

And that sucked. Large.

Sometimes my father recalls his days on a road crew when he reminisces about his youth.

He shoveled blacktop. All of his lanky 6'4" self, in his teens, spent countless days shoveling steaming blacktop in the summer sun. He describes it as backbreaking. I don't doubt him.

Dad's a funny one. He's job proud. He took the measure of his worth from how he spent his days. Before retirement, he was a teacher, an editor, a creative director, a special projects developer, and so much more. After earning yet another degree, this time an MBA, he landed at an investment firm. He developed a computer program that could parse out the values of the firm's clients and gear a specialized financial approach for each one.

I don't think it's unfair to say that my mid years spent as a trapeze artist proved difficult for Dad. He and his wife were infinitely interested in what their friends' children did for a living. When Dad asked me what he should tell people when they asked what I did for a living, I said, "Please tell them what I do, Dad."

"What is that exactly?"

I rolled my eyes. I should have been able to say that I was a cat burglar. Instead I said he should tell people I was a circus performer. I was an aerialist. And I was spectacular. I was really, really good at my job.

But Dad wasn't having it. He never saw me perform. And, to my knowledge, he never told anybody those exact words.

When my first novel was published, Joseph's first novel had been out for a year, and his fame had probably cloaked my smaller release. I can't imagine what any father might feel about a (my) sexually-charged novel about girls who grow into promiscuous young women. And often enough most readers, never mind dads, assume that fiction is somehow truth. So I don't know that my own hard earned first published novel made him very proud. But still.

He tried. He'd taught Shakespearean literature. He's an extraordinary and well-published poet. I have big boots to fill. My whole life. I haven't yet. But I've tried.

When I attended KCAI, Meg and I had a roommate who'd grown up rather privileged. I honestly don't know if what she told us was true. But she swore, that her mother swore, that Willy Nelson had been her mother's garbage man when he was young. Willy, if it's true, you rock. Willy, if it's not true, you rock.

It's probably fair to say that riding a garbage truck and slinging trash wasn't what Willy aspired to do all the rest of his days. Whether fact or fiction, he obviously doesn't do it now. And I'm betting that the woman at the airport who cleans the toilet stalls would rather be elsewhere. The person who picks grapes for 14 hours a day does it because of—or more likely *for*—someone else.

So long ago now, I met an American fine art painter living in Paris, the one I modeled for when I had no other work. I lay for hours in a relatively modest pose as he sketched and painted. He was an extraordinary realist. We chatted some. I daydreamed about my future. For some reason one day, he wanted to talk about work. What was the worst job I'd ever had?

At that point, I'd only had humble jobs besides modeling, all more or less equally bland, not much fun but fine, sorta. I hadn't liked having to wear a puffy plastic hair cap when I refreshed the salad bar on campus, I told him.

He laughed. He related. He was maybe seven or eight years older than I was, and he shared the story of his worst job. A small town Midwesterner, he'd had more than a few bad jobs. He'd worked in a chicken processing plant.

His worst job, he said, was working at an industrial bakery.

It didn't sound bad to me, not at all. Why? I'd asked him.

Well, he'd worked in The Hole. Nobody managed to work in The Hole for more than a week without quitting.

It smelled like yeast and the mildly sweet scent of just baked white bread.

And? I asked, trying not to move my face or mess up my hair as I lay there, breasts exposed, hips draped loosely with a bit of cotton sheet. Why was it so bad?

The Hole, he explained, was a completely underground three-story, open-to-the-rafters gigantic warehouse of a room, accessible only by a freight elevator, with no windows and no lighting save for a small singular hole in the ceiling.

And?

And he was the only person in it.

So?

His job was to stare up at the small, barely lit hole three stories up that provided work to him via a conveyor belt. Slowly, slowly, opened bags of buns, hotdog buns and hamburger buns—depending on the time of day—chugged down the skinny conveyor belt. His job was to put twisty ties on each and stack them on flats.

Um…

He had to wear a head to toe equivalent of a Hazmat suit. And the room was a 'cooling off' location after the industrial ovens. So no hot lights. And no air conditioning. His body hair, his sweat, none of it could contaminate the food product, so that's why he was covered in some fake fiber onesie head to toe, with a hood cinched around his face to cover his hair and short beard, even his eyebrows, only his nose and eyes uncovered. By himself. In the pitch black, save for the one singular hole in the ceiling.

He estimated it was 110 degrees inside The Hole. In the dark. On the dayshift. In the era before bottled water or the wisdom of hydration.

After his fourth or fifth shift, he'd started hallucinating, imagining the bags of buns as poop moving down a giant metallic creature's poop chute. He was the poop twisty-tie guy.

When he told me his work story, poking his head from behind his easel and canvas now and again, he said he still couldn't eat American white bread but related that he'd made it longer than any other worker in The Hole, nearly a month.

———

For some reason, associations die hard for me. I think 'conveyor belt' and I think about the worst conveyor belt job story I've ever heard. A guy I knew had only one arm. I don't think I can tell his story here with specific details but can summarize—he'd signed a nondisclosure agreement at the end of it all.

The guy had lost his other arm in a 'de-gloving' accident that happened while working for a major shipping company. He worked in the part of the warehouse that took large and heavy boxes, on a conveyor line, and strapped protective flexible metal straps around them with incredible speed, with an automated machine. The machine SCHOOOMP! sucked the box into its two-sided mouth, slapped on the straps, and SCHOOOMP! shot the box out the other end. Something had gone wrong with the machine, and the guy reached in to readjust a box. Down came the metal straps on top of his arm in a hair of a second and SCHOOOMP! out went his arm, strapped on top of the box. The machine yanked off his whole arm from his shoulder socket along with most of the skin on his back, hence the de-gloving term.

The red emergency stop button wasn't located where it was supposed to be. The guy ended up with over a million dollars. And one arm. He went into fine wine sales. He was amazing with a corkscrew and one arm, and every time he pulled a cork from a bottle he'd wedged between his legs, he would say, "Ahhh, I love that sound." He relished his new hobby. It wasn't a job. He just liked interacting with people, no longer confined to the inside of a shipping company warehouse.

I can't knock capitalism. I'm a consumer who lives in North America. While I know some people who live completely off the grid, harvest their own their energy and grow all their own food, hunt for their own protein, it's just not me. The work entailed in order to not work a job is too daunting.

Still, I can't help but think about how people get to 'where they are.' Americans' identities are so wrapped up in what they do for a living. How do those of us in menial positions define ourselves with any sort of confidence?

What if, just by accident, you landed a job as a mechanic's assistant when you were 15? And what if, by accident, you were impregnated by your boyfriend at 17? You kept crawling under those cars with a big belly, and then a second big belly two years later, because it worked best at the time, crawling under those cars because you didn't absolutely hate your job and you could help pay the bills?

Imagine if we really wanted to grow up to work in the sex trade or helm the midnight shift at 7-11. It's no one's aspiration—or at least not that person's parents' aspirations for their dear children. Yo! I want to grow up to be the woman who holds the sign on the highway work crew in August heat facing six lanes of oncoming traffic. I want to grow up to be a janitor at a high school. I want to be the detailing person at the car wash. I want to be the Zamboni driver—wait, everybody wants to be the Zamboni driver.

Some of us, a rare few, love what we do for a living. We *love* it. We relish it. We wake up each day so pumped to go to work we're bursting at the seams of our Hazmat suits. But those of us are the lucky minority. And getting to the current job that we truly love, well that involved a long-ass trail of undesirable jobs. But even when we've finally, magically landed the perfect, *perfect* job, it's not why we do it.

We do it for our daughters and sons. We do it to feel valued in our retirement community. We do it to do good, to heal, to protect, to first do no harm at the hospital. We do it so that we can grill eggplant slabs on Saturdays in our backyards for our husband's special lasagna. We do it so we can pay for our treasured rescue dog's expensive tooth cleaning. We do it with the yearning of slowing global warming or ridding humans of cancer or perpetuating a religion or becoming a sculptor who speaks to the human experience, who really connects to other people. Ambition is a human trait, a magnet and a driving force for many. We are motivated by something more than the work itself: our own legacy, small or large.

Usually though, nearly always, most of us work a job for the money. It's pretty simple. We need shelter and something to eat, and we want to give that to our loved ones too.

I'm on a kick lately. It's a promise I made to myself a few years ago. If I see something that's out of sorts in my home, I need to do something about it. I can't just walk by and a make a note-to-self about the stray Brussels sprouts leaves resting on the floor next to the garbage can or the dust bunny near the dog crate. I pick it up. I don't let my bed remain unmade. That kind of thing. I maintain some kind of order. I'm not sure if Marie Kondo has had something to do with my promise to myself or not. Hard to say. But lately I've been trying to extend that attitude, that not-ignoring, to other people who are working their jobs. I try to acknowledge and say thank you to the grumpy gas station attendant. I try to greet the front desk person at the library and muscle up some genuine warmth. If I have cash, I'll tip the bathroom attendant, sometimes the garbage men. Hey, one could be the next Willy.

That acknowledgement? It's all I ever wanted. That's only what somebody needed to show me in all those freak show jobs and menial jobs and subservient jobs. Just show me that you see me.

Alicia Keys understands, I think, with her song, "Good Job." The song is solid, but the accompanying video patched together in the days of a pandemic probably says much better what I'm after.

Good job. We see you. Or we're learning. We're learning
to see.

Before returning to teaching, while I worked on my novels and started a trapeze company, I bartended at a small restaurant with a brick floor and an outside patio where a wall of exotic, flowering ginger grew higher than my head. I had a following of regular customers.

One guy had been coming in for a month or two, usually at Happy Hour. He'd learned all of our names working there, loved to insert himself into our friendly rapport. While other employees goofed around at the wait station on the opposite end of the bar, the guy must have decided the timing was right.

'My sister knows your husband,' he told me.

Caught off guard, I feigned a simple sure-fine face. OK.

'He asked her out.'

Now what do I do? I must have picked up a rag and wiped something down.

'He took her for sushi on a date. He told her that you and he weren't close.'

I felt sick. I wondered how I'd get through my shift, the hours of the coming onslaught of college kids. My *husband* was going out on *dinner dates*.

The guy looked at the other employees. 'I think you should be with him," the customer said, indicating one of the workers. 'You two would be good together.'

I looked to the much younger man, nothing like my husband, and thought in the moment, honestly, Why the hell not? I could go low too.

It might have taken me a week to get him into bed.

Then

with Notes

Spring seeps slowly into Wisconsin. The season never arrives formally on a calendar; its warmth slips furtively in the back door in the northern states. Dogs and small children, lifting their noses to the wind, are the first to catch what must be an earthy smell of thaw, a slight weakening of winter's grasp. Days of premature, true heat are rarities full of great opportunities for those who have spent months watching the body's skin turn ashen as the sky, and days in

Milwaukee was an accidental city for me, one I probably wouldn't have chosen on my own had it not been for a guy. Tall, pale, blue-eyed. A guitarist-singer. We lived together for some time. He bought a tan Audi diesel four-door sedan from my brother-in-law and then never allowed me to drive the car. The boyfriend stored it in his parents' garage when he went on tour. And I took the bus. We broke up eventually, which is how I ended up living on my own, early April that bring near-tropical temperatures are considered actual blessings. When Milwaukee saw its thermometers ascend toward the heavenly eighties on April 7, 1991, the residents rejoiced.

I walked to work that night, a little before eight, remembering the dinner I'd shared with my mother at her house a few hours earlier, the chicken grilled over coals we'd managed to ignite without a male hand, the cheese muffins, the bottle of wine opened just to celebrate the weather. As I walked I marveled at the freedom of unrestricted movement; I wore no coat, no gloves, no boots. The day had been ideal in its leisure. I hoped the night of tending bar still ahead would be filled with good-tipping regulars. When fast footsteps approached from behind, I expected a friend to catch up with me, to retell his special day. But the footsteps and the warm weather did not bring a

with no car.

That month in April, as I had for many months, I worked a bartending gig I could walk to from my apartment near the university. Always the same schedule, week after week, same nights, same start time.

Cindy Crawford would star in her Pepsi ad in a year. Most all of us white girls aspired to her big hair, the tight clothes. Getting ready for work, at the same time I always did, I bent forward and upside-down, hair spraying my wavy long red-brown hair into an approximation of Cindy's hair. I pulled on black leggings, zipped up a skinny mini-pencil skirt, and topped it with a tight black T. I fed my cat, grabbed a fresh pack of smokes, my hairspray, my purse, and headed out my apartment building's door, same as I always did. Women's self defense classes then said that if you were a smoker, a lit cigarette made a good weapon. So I stood just friend. Instead, a rapist stole my mental grounding, my purse, and my body.

To avoid the details would be easy. But two individuals, the vice detectives, needed to know all that I remembered. And today, two years later, I still recall these details with perfect clarity. They form a part of the whole of me; they comprise a portion of an unalterable past that needs to be shared with many, for I have learned in my survival that if rape is ever to be seen as more than an impersonal figure, it must be made real for the graduate student, the CEO, the suburban housewife, the restaurant's dishwasher, the average person who hears or reads the statistics but cannot fathom the experience behind the numbers. Neither the punishment for the crime nor the reversal of blame—the all-too common courtroom scenario in which

outside on the apartment's walkway and lit one up. Like I always did. The cigarette usually lasted almost the length of the walk.

In a myriad of ways since the rape, my life has split itself in two. Before. And After.

I did the math. *That happened to me 29 years ago.* Of course now, I can no longer fathom how I thought it was fine to walk for blocks upon blocks in the dark on my own. I am compulsively driven to watch my women friends to their cars at night. I ask for texts when they reach their homes safely.

My calm reflection in "Then" belied a fear I hadn't completely shed, even two years post rape. Could I have done something differently? Could I have taken a cab to work?

the victim becomes the prosecuted—will change without awareness or understanding. To show, not report, seems to be key. In my case, a thousand words may speak louder than a newspaper picture.

I could not figure, at first, why the friend chose to throw an arm around my neck instead of my shoulder. With the sudden recognition that I would not hear the voice of a friend or coworker, my brain scrambled; synapses shut down. I did not understand, and felt the quick flush of blood to my face. I was tall and not weak. What was happening to me? How could this happen? Why? Only a minute before I saw so many people walking the same sidewalks, the sidewalks that ran in front of pretty duplexes and neat lawns and rose bushes guarded against the winter in blankets of mulch and white plastic garbage

Who was I? Why was I where I was, doing what I was doing? In Milwaukee, back then, I'd drifted into a sort of post-college complacency, but I believed in my autonomy through-and-through. It's possible I had low-grade depression. I hadn't wanted to break up with the musician. I found myself in a city that wasn't my own. I lived alone. But I had friends and an inherent belief that I could do pretty much whatever I wanted to. And I guess what I wanted to do in 1991 was make solid cash money and meet cute guys to help dull the ache the guitarist had left. He plucked my heartstrings hard enough that a few broke with a dissonant twang.

But before? I couldn't have imagined not being always and completely free. And after? After I have become most like my dog, or maybe my dog has become most like me.

A few months ago, I moved into an apartment

bags. I saw couples earlier, just a block back, holding hands, talking to each other and shuffling pale feet in sandals, the scuffling and flip-flopping noises comforting and familiar. Where were all the people?

The sky glowed deep lavender. The streetlights sputtered an early orange. The arm around my neck was warm and sinewed; its attached body must not have been chilled with fright nor weak and unresolved.

Something hard hit the back of my head near the small flat spot I'd retained from bouncing off a bed backwards in childhood. Something was happening.

Something is wrong. The arm is part of a he, and he wants my purse. I am being mugged. Drop the purse, my faltering brain tells the hand that holds it. Only money. Only, only—what is there? Credit cards and passport and lipstick and two dollars and the new coin purse and a photo of my boyfriend

building again, the first since my Milwaukee years. The New Orleans building is an old elementary school that's been lovingly and beautifully renovated into apartments after having sat empty for more than a decade due to Hurricane Katrina. I have 13.5' ceilings and breathing space. They kept the original hardwood floors. The psychic vibe is informed by former students and teachers as well as the following years of empty and calm obsolescence. It's a good fit at this point in my life, post-divorce.

My loyal companion, all of eight and a half pounds, Fry (technically Fritz Friday—he came with the name, being a rescue dog, a long-legged red deer chihuahua who's been at my side for nearly 11 years now) has endured too many moves of late. I feel for the little guy. He glues himself to me when he's able, keeps me in eyesight when he can't physically touch me.

alongside old movie stubs and mints. The hand obeys. Drop the purse and he will let go, pick it up, leave. And keys. And ID with my address on it.

My purse thumps to the sidewalk. Where are the couples now? Couldn't they hear my yell, eking through my constricted throat—I can't breathe won't he let go and take my purse—can't someone hear my plastic bottle of hairspray clattering on the cement? He, oh god he doesn't want the purse I dropped the purse "my purse is over there I dropped my purse" I squeeze out I can't breathe please your other arm is wrapped around my chest I can't raise my arms I can't move them the sky is changing black red those are my ankles dragging on the sidewalk I see blood why am I going up this driveway I can't see my neck my throat hurts why.

I am so comfortable lounging in a preawakening dream in the morning. The

He lost three teeth recently. His muzzle has gone white as well as two sweet half moons under his big eyes. His ears rise, giant furry triangles, from his apple head. He can rotate his huge ears independently of one another. He's smart as shit.

And he is aware of his own safety. He is aware of our safety.

I chose this old school apartment building because I knew the neighborhood and because it had gated, off-street parking. It allows dogs. Fry loves nothing more than to wander freely, smelling everything he can. But he doesn't wander far. Inside, he bounds up the huge staircases of the old school and runs with abandon down the long hallways, but he won't race far from me when outside. Last week, Fry and I went out back for his last pee, nearly 12:30 at night. I am vigilant, always, at such an hour. And so is Fry. He growled and started barking smooth bed sheets, worn from three children and Mom's iron, are tucked around my neck. I dream of grilling chicken and laughing with my mother; of thick cream I'd poured in my coffee in the morning; of high school graduation; of the big foot-kicked dent in my eighth grade locker; of the family dog that died, that leapt over the backyard fence one final time, staggering away on arthritic legs to die in Forest Park across so many lanes of traffic; of Chicago; of the house with the wood paneled playroom in River Forest; of the black spot on the wall I made my father check before bedtime—I was so certain it was a bug, wavering with the vision that would soon need glasses, a bug that sat in wait for me to fall asleep, cleaning antennae with spiked front legs; of the giant slide that Dad failed to catch me at the end of, even though he said he would—he promised he would catch me; of falling,

from a distance at something I couldn't see but he could smell, or maybe hear.

I thought he'd picked up the scent of a possum or maybe a feral cat, but that's actually not what he noted. He tried to tell me that the rear automated parking gate was stuck open. He trotted forward and indicated with his nose. He stopped in place, turned his head to me, then held his ground and indicated once more the wide-open gap in the always-closed fence line.

My dog, as much as I am, is aware of our safety. We are both always on the lookout. I can say with certainty that I will forever carry the burden of my vigilance. It is my albatross. I grew it like a monstrous limp appendage from the back of my strangled neck. It will always be there. It will not atrophy. It will not go away.

falling. And I am rising. I see smoke from a backyard grill. I see asphalt rooftops and brick chimneys. I see a body, my body, in a driveway between two Milwaukee duplexes. I see red hair and a black T shirt and white flesh dirtied, soiled, bloody. I am not dreaming in bed.

The air was so cold, so spiked with pain, that when I drew in the breath my lungs whistled. I felt grass under the backs of my hands. Where were my hands? They rested, curled at my sides, turned up in unconscious submission. Warm. The air was warm; my lungs seemed so cold. Something was wet, oh please no. My lower back, my ass, my thighs. My clothes, where were my clothes? Shoved down, away, around my knees. I did not want to open my eyes. I knew everything already that I did not want to see. I'd been trampled into a strip of grass and asphalt, it seemed, smashed and split like some yielding peach. Ripped flesh

Except with family or very close friends, I've been reluctant to call what happened to me that night, as I lay dying, an out-of-body experience, but I have no other words for it. To acknowledge it in a public forum is to risk embarrassment or maybe even ridicule. I must not have wanted to go there, to say such things when in graduate school. I wrote the essay with zero intention of sending it out into the world. I wrote cathartically for myself and to offer up some explanation for the new person I'd become, the new person I'd reinvented in New Orleans, to my fellow students and new friends.

Then why now?

I don't know that I'm capable of seeing my own changes specifically over the decades. I can't say with certainly when I developed the more pronounced crinkle torn. My own urine and blood and excrement cooled on my skin.

Nothing focused. Where were my contacts? I rolled my eyes to catch the lenses; they were up there between the hard orb and lid somewhere, weren't they? No. I could see almost nothing. But there, who was that, there on the sidewalk? He was tall and dark and I could not tell if the figure was looking back at me, my legs twisted unnaturally on the driveway, one foot turned inward, the other out. Or was the person strolling by, strolling by in the April night?

I was alive. I needed help. I could walk, I thought. I pulled up my skirt, my leggings, my underwear. I could smell the insides of my body and the acrid tang of a stranger's semen. I could run. I picked up all that was left, clutched the bottle of hairspray against my chest, ran blindly across the street, up onto a gray porch, rang

under my left eye than the right when I smile, or exactly when my spine began to register discomfort in up-dog.

I don't believe that time heals all wounds. It can't. But time, when we're lucky, happens.

At some point I learned to care less about how other people judged me and tried harder to connect on a meaningful level with friends and strangers alike. Yeah, this revolting, violent crime changed my life. Maybe if I share it, in its gory detail, somebody else will relate. And that counts for something. Maybe that's actually something important.

Probably? I'm living alone again because I am divorced. I've been considering my life in different ways than I had for so long.

But I did not die. Not then, in 1991, and not now, in 2019. If you, survivor of rape, are alive and reading the doorbell. I rang and rang and no one answered. Had to get help. Call an ambulance. I ran to the next house and then the next. Why was nobody home, settled in an easy chair in front of a TV, laughing at sitcoms? Where were all the people I might see behind screen doors going back into a kitchen for leftovers? Two blurry figures—I could make out two—were moving down the sidewalk. Two would be safe. Two could not be one, Him. I asked for help.

———

I told my story, as best I could, to the detectives who came to the hospital to interview me, to dig out the details like bits of meaty walnut from the shell. They questioned while I waited for the special doctor, a male doctor, the professional, the trained rape physician arriving from someplace else to use numbered swabs and numbered slides and

this, you can also make it through to the other side of the page.

———

I never thanked the couple who brought me into their apartment and called the police. I couldn't see them very well. I stank. They let me use their bathroom. I don't know if I left blood-smeared toilet paper everywhere or tried to flush it away. I don't know that I asked their names. The woman cried for me. They were kind people.

Thank you, good couple. Thank you.

———

Patience is not one of my virtues. I believe, fully and absolutely, that it's supposed to be my life lesson this go-around on earth. I'm supposed to swallow the big horse pill of my impatience every day like a vitamin, and I'm supposed to smear numbered plastic baggies and scissors and syringes and tweezers and tongs and fine-toothed combs to collect clothing and pubic hair and blood and body fluid. All were physical evidence.

The special doctor did not arrive for three hours. I was not allowed to urinate or wash in any manner. While shaking in wait, I listened to my mother cry by my side. I called and left a message on my boyfriend's answering machine. I called information for my credit cards' 800 numbers. My mother called family.

I did not know why, until I was cleaned and given fresh second-hand clothes much later, why my mother sobbed when she looked at me. I couldn't see her reaction clearly; my contacts were unmistakably gone. When I finally went to a bathroom to change, passing a nurses' station where white-uniformed women laughed and told jokes amongst themselves, I

patience all over my body every morning out of the shower like sunscreen. I will myself not to honk when sitting behind somebody still texting, head down, five seconds after the light has turned green. I will myself not to sigh audibly in the grocery line when a senior citizen decides to write a check.

I am not a native New Orleanian. Those who are have been weaned on patience. So many wait in the heat or rain for perpetually late busses and streetcars and for their number to blink on above one of the windows at the DMV. They wait for street crews to fix potholes, for power crews to restore electricity after tropical storms, for their names to be called in traffic court. They wait hours past the advertised start time for Rebirth to play at the Maple Leaf. They wait for the second line parade to make it down the road before they can finish their drive saw. I stared into the mirror above the shallow handicap sink. Most of the capillaries, the little veins beneath the skin's surface that bring a shy blush to the cheeks or an angry redness to a forehead, had burst. Crimson blood dotted my entire face, trapped inside. I would later learn that these broken capillaries, along with the purple and blue bruises on my neck, were signs morticians most often saw. Strangulation causes eyes to bulge and their surface to distend; my soft contact lenses had flipped inside-out and into the grass.

Forensic science[edit]
Petechiae on the face and conjunctiva (eyes) can be a sign of a death by asphyxiation, particularly when involving reduced venous return from the head (such as in strangulation). Petechiae are thought to result from an increase of pressure in the veins of the head and hypoxic damage to endothelia of blood vessels.[8]

to their niece's graduation. Life in New Orleans is one long series of exercises in patience. Those born here accept it as a tool for managing the simple same ol'-same ol' everyday.

I wish I could say I'm making strides in my ability to incorporate patience. But I'm not. I try, but to no avail, and it occurs to me that I have the rape to blame, at least in part.

Waiting for that doctor in Milwaukee that April night, I grappled with intensely complex emotions, complex realizations about my life and how it would change.

But as I sat in the isolated single waiting room, something became abundantly clear: I had made it out alive. Time for me to get on with it, whatever "it" was.

I don't think I'm the only one who's experienced a personal tipping point. Life Before Dad Died. Life After Dad Died. Life Before Breast

Petechiae can be used by police investigators in determining if strangulation has been part of an attack. The documentation of the presence of petechiae on a victim can help police investigators prove the case. [9] Petechiae resulting from strangulation can be relatively tiny and light in color to very bright and pronounced. Petechiae may be seen on the face, in the whites of the eyes or on the inside of the eyelids.

———

In the immediate weeks following the rape, I did not know how I could live. My mind moved over its stored thoughts and absorbed new information randomly. I wondered whether ants might carry my shriveled contacts back to their queen, how I'd been left for dead, why we ate eggs at Easter, how I'd need to wait the necessary six months for my HIV test. I could only visit my apartment with family and dashed around, searching for things I did not need to assure myself that

Cancer. Life After Breast Cancer. Here in New Orleans, ours have become short acronyms: PK. Pre-Katrina. AK. After Katrina.

In 1991, I needed, I desperately needed, to snap my fingers and reside in the future. I needed to be living someplace safe, and normal, and I needed to do it in a heartbeat.

But I couldn't. I couldn't see the future, never mind get there instantaneously. I wanted everything to hurry up as much as I wanted everything that had just happened to be put away into storage, into some cedar closet in my brain that almost never got opened. But I had more waiting, a lot more waiting, still to do.

Because of the physicality of my rape, there was a very good possibility of my having been infected with HIV if the rapist were a carrier. And in '91, it took six months of waiting for the only test available back then to determine whether they still existed unchanged, the way I remembered them: a floral scarf, a set of antique claw-and-ball feet, the collection of cobalt bottles. I no longer cared whether my cat ate his properly-balanced food or cheap generic, or whether clothes were folded straight from the dryer or forgotten for days to wrinkle. I imagined Him flipping through my passport, noting the Paris ink stamp, figuring which key belonged to what lock, finding my Planned Parenthood card and the address of my father in St. Louis.

But later, in the slow sharing of my story, I found myself, my anger, my hope for some future. I told all who would listen my tales of the aftermath.

A police department telephone operator was the one to inform me that no record of an April 7 rape on Cramer Street existed. I asked to speak to the detectives. I was told that what had happened could not be

or not my body had begun to attempt to fight against a foreign invader of extreme might.

To this day, they were the longest six months of my life.

———

My impatience clearly has some systemic roots that don't make a lot of sense if you don't know my history. If you don't know that my entire life view shifted in one night, an unusually balmy night, in Milwaukee. Now, I want what is *right* to always happen, and I want it to happen right now. I just can't help it.

As for the classification of what happened to me on April 7, 1991, the fact that my face was mottled horrifically, my neck bruised, an egg-size bump sprouted from my head, my body soiled, my vagina and anus torn and bloodied, semen collected, countless swabs used to preserve evidence, technically classified as rape yet since I was not actually conscious during the event— because I saw nothing other than the color of an arm. The crime was to be labeled a strong-arm robbery. A mugging was what police related to the concerned women of the neighborhood when they called inquiring about the police cars and ambulances. My testimony of the events was not enough; my file would not move to the rape cabinet until the physical evidence was returned from the lab in Madison. Of course, they said, the procedures used to preserve the physical evidence were very good. The contents of my baggies could last indefinitely. They might reach the top of the stack for processing in as little as six months. Until that time, technically only my purse had been taken from me.

The day following the rape, I called all the television news stations and ankles scraped, multiple bruises noted across my legs, buttocks, and back, I wasn't technically raped, or not by police standards at that time. This, looking back with some modicum of objectivity, blows my mind. If you're shot in the back of the head, and you couldn't see the perpetrator, were you not shot? If fire fell from the sky and set you aflame but you didn't see the source, were you not burned? Or would test kits be the only things to determine what happened at some miscellaneous future date?

I am obviously still angry. I am angry at The System. And I am perpetually impatient in a world where survivors must prove themselves first. How can it be that for so long, so few actually listened to what we've tried to say? I've been waiting for 29 years.

three newspapers. All but one, the smallest and most local of the newspapers, told me bluntly that they believe my 'accident' was not newsworthy. But there were so many single female students in my neighborhood, I said. They should know that He was out there.

A large corporation owned the apartment building in which I lived. I called a managing supervisor and told her my story. Please would you change the locks on the building's outer door, I asked, if only for the safety of the other women? No, I was not living in my apartment any longer. The corporation at last changed the locks two and a half weeks later under my threat to paste flyers in the hallways, warning tenants that a rapist had keys to the building. The corporation in turn threatened to sue me for failure to fulfill the terms of my lease. I moved out of town.

How many logs on the pyre does the media need to report rape as something worthy of their broadcast, their publication? Series of rapes, only, it seems. Many upon many. All these years and several more progressive, assertive, and wise generations later, has enough actually changed?

What happened to me should never descend on any other family member, any other friend. Any other stranger. Not here in New Orleans, not in Omaha or Kansas City or Asheville or Seattle or Portland or Boston. Not in Toronto. Not in Vancouver. Not in Madrid. Not in Cape Town. Not in San Miguel. Not in Warsaw. Not in Anchorage. Not in Beijing.

But it will.

My experience was unique. All rapes are utterly unique.

A Milwaukee friend called several months after my move to let me know that a serial rapist had been striking women within a six block radius of where I had been attacked. News reports had suddenly surfaced after number 12. I don't know what number I am or if my case report is included. The police have yet to apprehend the rapist, and incoming freshmen and the nearby university are not warned of any problems occurring around the campus.

This February I found out from a New Orleans friend that seventeen women had been raped at last count in the Marigny. I mention the fact to many. Beyond a man who works with the police, no one I told had heard. I suppose this city as well believes that rape is not a newsworthy subject, or that if the crime is left unpublicized, he may make a mistake and get careless with the next mother, sister, or

They are not a cookie-cutter happening, despite the fact that statistics provide evidence to the contrary in terms of baseline numbers and regularity of occurrences. What about all the women, all the humans—rape is most certainly not gender specific—who see no point in reporting the crime at all? What would happen to the statistics if there were some way of counting the silent people the way the government can count soldiers with PTSD?

I still remember the sound of running footsteps behind me on the sidewalk, a sound that has sparked panic for 29 years now. I remember the feel of the arms thrown across my chest and around my throat, the weight of the stranger heavy on my back. I remember, with immense regret, not being able to reach my hand, with its lit cigarette, to the rapist's bare arm.

But most often now, I remember how what

wife. The girlfriend may get a good look and survive to tell the detectives.

Statistics show that with the lengthening of the day, the tilt of our world towards the sun, warmer weather stirs in men an increased tendency towards violence. Recent figures indicate that winter is waning early this year.

happened spurred me to understand that I'd been given another chance.

More breaths. More heartbeats.

That extra chance, it counted for something. I could still do more with my borrowed time. I started writing as though my life depended on it. And probably? It did. I owed myself a new path. Go, I told myself. Flourish. Despite it all. Find courage.

Go.

The man who saw me through the rape to the other side moved to New Orleans with me when I started graduate school. He said he would follow me around the world if need be. He cooked delicious Indian food and made amazing art. He just never got into self-promotion. I once dragged a huge folding screen that he'd painted on both sides to local New Orleans galleries trying to get him attention. He couldn't bring himself to go with me to talk about his work.

Some years after we'd broken up and Joseph and I had married, I heard my ex had followed a woman to Alaska. I think he ended up back in New Orleans a while later again with a different woman, but he'd gone halfway around the globe, nearly, supporting a partner.

A good 15 years later, one of my best graduate school friends and I reconnected. She and I stood in the looming weight of the past in the National WWII Museum in New Orleans, a propeller plane hanging overhead from the ceiling. She confessed to me that she'd made out with my ex. She knew I wouldn't care about it anymore, she said, but that he'd been so handsome she couldn't help herself.

I suppose trolls somewhere or those afflicted with schadenfreude might say I got what I deserved, to be betrayed after I'd betrayed another. But I never cheated on my ex-boyfriend. Joseph and I didn't hook up till I'd called it off with the artist.

I'd really loved that folding screen. The gold leaf background. The painted superhero in flight.

I Got the Dog

In my mind's eye, somewhere in the Midwest, there existed a place to start over. I thought I needed to wash myself clean of my husband's cheating mire and the thick New Orleans humidity that associatively conjured only misery. I sought a place with actual seasons. I hadn't experienced an autumn or full winter in decades. Truly.

KCAI, the art college I'd finished at in the late 80s, pulsed in a quiet way from afar. I knew the lay of the land, albeit in a cursory way. Kansas City pleased my color sensibilities, a vigorous blue dot island in the sea of a red state, holding firm, deep liberal roots enforcing the city's right to be weird like an Austin cousin.

Kansas City hadn't been my immediate choice after so many years in New Orleans though. Family lived in St. Louis: Dad and his wife Mary Anne; Mom; sister Emily and her husband and three kids. Why not wrap myself up in the robe of familial love? I felt as pummeled as a prizefighter who'd lost in the final round.

As duped as the kid who'd wagered and lost her lunch money at morning recess. I didn't know what end was up. Head North, I thought. Pack up the dog and just go. It was the direction that could bring some comfort. I had savings enough from my half of the sales of our properties to live on for maybe two years, if I were careful.

I also considered running away to someplace where nobody could find me, ever. Bali or Brazil. Barcelona.

Or just retreat to St. Louis.

For me, when the rug was yanked out, I sought the familiar rather than the new. I wish I'd had the wherewithal to head to Zimbabwe. But I chickened out. Mom's Alzheimer's diagnosis had much to do with my driving up I-55 and back into the stomping grounds of my teen years.

To where I lost my virginity on a couch in a house on San Bonita. To where I used to sunbathe on the seminary grounds with lemon juice in my hair. To where I learned how to golf and play tennis and field hockey and run the hurdles and high jump and help tap a keg at a homecoming float decorating party. Where I learned how to drive. Thirty-four years later, I'd landed back in my high school city.

Unable, however, to stomach living on top of my former teenage self like a translucent vellum overlay, I couldn't bring myself to choose Clayton as an option. I considered buying a house in one of several more unconventional neighborhoods, maybe South Grand or Soulard. St. Louis has an abundance of turn-of-the-century, solid brick, two- and three-story houses. Hardwood floors, high ceilings, fireplaces. Aesthetically, I could see myself in one.

A few years earlier, Joseph and I had bought my mom the small brick house she currently lives in, at least for a little while longer. A small down payment, a small monthly mortgage. She needed a decent place to live, and we could manage it. So in the interim of my move out of New Orleans and into somewhere I didn't exactly yet know, I moved temporarily into the guest bedroom at Mom's while my remaining earthly belongings went into storage. Fry and I slept side-by-side and greeted Mom every morning while she made her coffee.

Post 'dissolution of movables' with Joseph, I joined the local YMCA in St. Louis and took all kinds of group classes. I used the elliptical machines. I found a realtor willing to show me houses in my possible neighborhoods. I cleaned moldy produce out of my mother's refrigerator drawers and took her to lunch, usually at our favorite authentic Mexican place. I visited with my dad and his wife, made them dinner, went to movies with my sister Emily. We went to see *The Wife*, starring Glenn Close, and afterwards ate Korean barbeque. We talked about what had happened to my marriage, what had happened to me, my inability to see what seemed to have been coming down the pike for years. I watched innocuous television at night and, as Colin Hay sings, I waited for my real life to begin. I don't know how many times I listened to that song or how many times I cried.

> Any minute now, my ship is coming in
> I'll keep checking the horizon . . .
> I already have a plan
> I'm waiting for my real life to begin
> When I awoke today, suddenly nothing happened
> But in my dreams, I slew the dragon
> And down this beaten path, up this cobbled lane
> I'm walking in my old footsteps, once again

The song destroyed me. It still does. The worst part about the beautiful lyrics was that they reminded me that I no longer had a 'you.' Not anymore. Hay sings, "*And you say, be still my love.*" I didn't have that You. Somebody stole him out from under me. Or maybe the You just floated away on an air current I couldn't catch. Maybe greed ate the You. Maybe lust swallowed the You.

Nobody called me 'my love' anymore.

In subtle weekly increments, St. Louis began to feel more and more ill-fitting. I couldn't actually put my finger on what specifically factored into the reaction other than a lingering long-ago sensation of having wanted to desperately escape. St. Louis was, is, a perfectly comfortable city. A good place to raise children, I suppose. But I'd never had kids. I didn't often eat toasted ravioli. Even though I know the zoo to be a quality institution, wild animals in enclosures make my heart hurt severely, and I wouldn't be able to bring myself to visit them ever. Yes, the Arch rises shiny over the river and downtown, and the art museum kicks ass. But St. Louis wasn't going to work for me.

My psychic-medium sister Meg said I should rent. That I should consider someplace else other than St. Louis. She saw me on a second floor balcony.

Mom and I weren't butting heads, per se, but living with Mom at my age came straight from the script of the genius flick *Bridesmaids*. Only I was even older than Kristen Wiig's character. Talk about a reason to cry listening to "Waiting for my Real Life to Begin."

Left to her own devices, Mom would opt for marzipan for breakfast, candy corn for lunch, and waffles for dinner. Then she'd tell me that she knows she should eat more protein. I quit force-feeding her salads. She usually remembered that I didn't eat coffeecake. We found a decent middle ground. We did jigsaw puzzles together and watched Jeopardy. But I had to get outta there.

A strange opportunity arose as if by magic. The upper duplex unit above one of Meg's best friends, who lived in Kansas

City, would soon be available. The professional ball player who lived there had been traded. The place, almost brand new and techy-advanced, had a two-car basement garage slot just for me, a bone-dry storage unit, solar panels, deep core heating and cooling, an induction stovetop, huge pantry-laundry, two bedroom, two and a half baths, Google Fiber, and was all-inclusive. Nice big second floor covered balcony out front with room for me to put up my hanging chair come spring. Plant herbs, write, and get on with things somehow, not for the first time in my life.

Because why not Kansas City? Mid-point between Nebraska and Meg's family and St. Louis with Emily's family and our parents, how bad could it be?

Pricilla and Elvis lived in the first floor unit. She chose their pseudonyms for these pages because she couldn't pass up a chance for a bit of levity when giving me permission to relay the months to come.

Pricilla, Meg's dear friend, and I were born in the same year. Pricilla is slender and athletic and rocks a tight pair of jeans and boots with a wide leather belt. Some might call her off-puttingly direct. I found her intelligence and take-no-bullshit approach to life welcome, a wedge of lemon in cool water. Pricilla has a tonally low speaking voice. She is divorced and has a grown son.

Elvis also has a couple grown kids and is divorced. He is small in stature, huge in heart. Ruddy, affable, and Texan, he drives a monstrous pickup truck you have to climb into. He parks it, two inches to spare, in his designated slot in the underground garage, backing it in as easily as his Hot Wheels corvette into a cut-out shoebox.

Pricilla and Elvis welcomed me with genuine warmth.

———

The physical strain of a long distance move can turn even the most stalwart of people to porridge. Only a few options exist for those of us with moderate means. I got some estimates that made me realize something. When a company hires a new employee from out of state, and that company offers to pay for the long distance move, that company really, *really* wants that employee. We're lookin' at 25k, easy, for a just-married couple, 35k or more for a family of four.

I couldn't afford a moving company to do it all for me.

You know how long it takes to wrap Christmas presents. Multiply that by a hundred if you want your valuables to survive. I lost my mind in New Orleans before that first move north, packing and boxing breakables for weeks on end. Styrofoam sheets, wadded newsprint, foam plate dividers, bubble wrap of various sizes, six different sizes of flat boxes needing assembly, rolls upon rolls of packaging tape, tape dispensers, Sharpies, moving blankets, more tape, rolls of giant saran wrap, styrofoam peanuts.

The chaos looks, at first, as though it might be contained, but not a chance. Maybe two weeks into the packing, seven days a week, I'd resorted to finding the humor in the moment. I took photos of my perspiring self in a blue exercise tank top with my head enrobed in bubble wrap, initiating my Bubble Wrap Madonna Portrait Series, a la Cindy Sherman. I never thought something was so funny, my blue eyes oh-so demure beneath my modest hood of bubble wrap, my face dripping with sweat. I cracked myself up till I cried, and then I looked around again at all the work still to be done and laughed and cried some more. I sent the photos to my sisters, who appreciated my sense of humor. They understood my emotional degeneration.

After loading up at my storage unit in St. Louis, I drove one moving truck. My brother-in-law Lance drove the other. In the rain and into the dark. The next day we unloaded with the help of many careful hired young hands. My sisters helped on both ends, as did my niece and nephew.

And so. Well. I'd made it to Kansas City. Hands on hips in my new duplex, I stood in the middle of a maze of boxes and blanketed furniture and looked around. The move was finished, sorta. My real life could begin any day.

I waited and watched for that day and started walking my new neighborhood, autumn dancing around in her bright burlesque costumes. Photo op piled on top of the next. I couldn't stop taking pictures of the season I'd missed for so long. After decades of tropical green, I slavered like a lapsed priest at blaze red maples, bright yellow ashes, orange sumacs, blushing sassafras. Cascades of golden ginko leaves, all dropping in a single day. Black tupelo turning purple, glossy sweetgum going maroon. The trees and bushes stripteased me silly.

And the air! Wind, actual wind that wasn't generated by a hurricane. In Kansas City, the wind carried the scent of rolled hay off the prairies, wood smoke from down the road, sometimes kielbasa grilling on Elvis' porch downstairs. The sky was taller, bluer than in New Orleans, the circling hawks more majestic.

I could do outdoors. Indoors, though, sucked. I hadn't really considered what I had left or what I had lost, both the physical and the untouchable, until I began to unpack after the months of storage. St. Louis had been a better distraction than I'd realized. A pair of gray and black lamp bases made me miss the white swan-necked ones Joseph had chosen. The china set I'd inherited from my grandmother went into the pantry cupboards, clinking out echoes of the Thanksgiving meals I'd prepared and hosted in our old New Orleans house, never to be repeated. Each object coerced a memory whether I wanted it to or not. Two dining armchairs out of four. Split-up collections of framed photography. Only some of the rugs that Fry had rubbed his jaw on after finishing a bone. Bed linens stained with ink from Joseph's last tattoo. Mismatched glasses. Literally half of one sofa comprised of two identical parts. Would Joseph spoon his new woman on his half? Change his baby son's diapers there while listening to the playlists he and I had compiled? With each unwrapping of an object, the fling of another sheet of crumpled newsprint, I felt the pinprick, over and over.

I'd been banking on Pricilla becoming my new friend, somebody to show me the ropes of a city I minimally remembered. A gifted photographer and travel guide of photography excursions to exotic and distant locales, Pricilla remained forever and always herself. If I'd been a tomboy as a kid, Pricilla had stayed one as an adult. One evening late into October after I'd finally finished unpacking, she and Elvis invited me down for champagne and snacks. They were getting ready to go to a costume party. Pricilla asked if I could maybe assist with their makeup. I brought down eyeliner and shadow, lipstick, powder. I loved embellishing faces, always have.

They'd decided to dress as Dia de la Muerte skeleton peeps, had gone all out on their costumes. Pricilla had found some kind of Mexican dirndl Frida Kahlo get-up I helped yank her into, *Gone with the Wind* bedpost style. Elvis wore a black suit and hat studded with metal bones on the headband, a skeleton vest. I wet faux tattoo appliques and carefully held them to Pricilla's chin and under Elvis' eyes. Something kinda cool happens when near strangers are forced to put their faces close together. I'm guessing makeup artists and hairdressers experience it all the time. Elvis and Pricilla had to trust my efforts with their Halloween makeup, and I had to grow comfortable enough to get physically close, touching Pricilla's eyebrows to darken her eyelids black, holding Elvis' chin in my hand to raise his head higher.

After a couple glasses of champagne, we considered the results. They both looked freakish and spectacular. I took photos of the Presleys in our communal hallway and off they went to the party. I felt like we'd broken the ice.

And so the weeks ticked on. Thanksgiving cast an imposing shadow in the ensuing, shortening days. Pricilla and I decided we should host for the holiday, turn the whole duplex into a big open house. Meg and her family would stay with me, and Pricilla's family would stay with them. We'd have some meals downstairs, some up. Friends from town would come and go. The leaves had dropped from all the neighborhood's deciduous trees. The squirrels madly collected and buried acorns in the back and side yards, fattening themselves up on birdseed beneath the feeders. The Thanksgiving holiday functioned as my goal to have my new place ready to show, ready to share with others: see, I'm an independent and functioning woman. I haven't lost my mind. Sure, I haven't written a ton yet, but I will. I can feel it. I'll set up right there in front of the big window and write for days on end. After Thanksgiving. That's where you'll find me.

And then. About that time, a couple weeks before the turkey celebration, the Things began.

In New Orleans, I'd always let Fry out into the back walled courtyard, unleashed. No need for one. No stray dog could scale the wall, topped with spikes, and no other creatures, save for the occasional confused juvenile possum, dared enter the space.

Sure, the lizards hung out, sometimes a frog or two. Lots of butterflies came through on their migration path. But in all the years I'd had Fry, I'd never needed to put a leash on him. In the early months after adopting him as a rescue dog, I'd tried but he hated his harness, hated being on a leash, slunk down the sidewalk trying to tangle himself up in my legs, his tail curled tightly against his otherwise exposed anus. He never peed, never stopped to sniff a bush. He learned, though, that his backyard haven was something to be protected. It was *his.* He barked like he had rabies at leashed dogs passing on the sidewalk on the other side of the wall, a ridge of hair down his back standing on end. And then he'd look over his shoulder at me. See? he said with his brown eyes. I'm protecting us.

My Kansas City apartment came with a backyard. Two of the three sides were fenced with a standard-height wooden fence. The third sported a shorter fence and gate with slats farther apart, more of a decorative side that included slab stone steps and a stone retaining wall. Pricilla and Elvis didn't have any pets. They never used the yard, so it would be perfect for Fry. There were no bushes or trees. Just four corners, a fence, and a flat square of grass.

Fry and I got there by going out my back door off the pantry and heading down two flights of deck stairs. Easy peasy. Out he went onto the grass while I usually held back, barefoot no matter the weather in solidarity with my dog, standing on the lowest step. He sniffed the perimeter, always, and found some new spot to mark.

Fry has had very limited exposure to cold weather. He's not a fan. He has short hair. He doesn't even weigh 9 pounds. One morning we opened the back door and headed down the deck stairs when we discovered that the midway landing wasn't constructed of wood. It had frozen overnight, and the slick surface of the perma-plastic fake lumber had turned into a slip-n-slide. Fry went down the stairs first, hit the landing, and lost his footing. He slid towards the edge of the drop-off, the railing not nearly low enough to stop a skidding chihuahua. I scrambled after him, slamming onto my ass, but caught him in time.

I tried not to freak out too badly. Of course, like the highway signs say, bridge freezes before road. An elevated expanse of plastic wood would certainly ice before the ground. I stood carefully, hanging onto the rail, and set Fry aright onto the first real wooden step. We descended with caution and then Fry went on his morning exploration. The frost on the grass seemed to pique his curiosity. I turned my attention to my I-Phone, rubbing my sore ass, and dialed an early bird friend in California. We caught up while Fry wandered the square of lawn, mincing his prancing pony way around. My gaze drifted to the bare trees past the yard, across the nearby neighbors' back lawns, taking in the architecture of Kansas City that had nothing to do with New Orleans' at all.

And then I saw it.

"Oh my god!" I said to my California friend on the phone. "Oh my god!!"

"What?" he asked, not yet alarmed.

"Oh my god!! What the fuck is that!?!"

"What?" he asked with more interest.

"Oh, fuck! There's more than one! What *IS* that? Oh my god!! What are those?!"

"Take a video. Wait. You can't with me on the phone. Take photos. *What!?*"

"Is that a *COUGAR?!?!*" I asked. "*What the fuck IS that?!?!*"

I glanced around the green square of yard to locate Fry. Obliviously, he took a dump in the far corner. I focused in on the neighbor's rear garage two lots away. On the slanted rooftop stood what looked to me, exactly, like a wild cougar.

Dun-colored, slinky, huge, and crouching, it turned its head my direction. A second entity, the same color but much smaller, scrambled up after it onto the rooftop.

I tried to take photos, but the significantly bigger first one had already escaped down a tree. The smaller one paused to note my presence and human voice then leapt away, bounding over a chain link fence with ease and disappearing behind heavy brush.

I managed two blurry photos of the second animal on the rooftop. Opinions were mixed. I sent the photos out to a number of people, including some seriously in the know. My brother-in-law Lance, via sister Meg, swore it was a fox.

"But it's bigger than a fox, and dun-colored," I countered. "And the first one I didn't get a photo of was probably 30 pounds bigger than that one. It was huge!"

"They come in that color," he said. Lance had grown up in rural Nebraska. I wanted to believe him. I did. Two foxes were better than two cougars. But do foxes climb easily onto rooftops? There weren't any lean-tos against the garage. Can a fox get onto the roof of a garage that's at least 11 feet off the ground with complete ease? And why would it? Why would a *pair*—let's be romantic and call them a mating couple—of foxes purposely get on top of a garage roof with massive effort on their part? For what?

But I knew the answer. Cougars, or the biggest fucking foxes I've ever seen in my life, wanted to know what there was to eat. My neighborhood bordered a beautiful, hilly, and wild walking park with hiking paths and lots of nooks and dens for wildlife. A pair of somethings had gone in hunt for breakfast.

Fry would not be breakfast.

I caught my breath. After the threat had gone the opposite direction, Fry sniffed around the yard. He smelled something on the ground then ate it. "Stop it!" I scolded and walked to him through the frost melting to dew on the lawn. "Spit it out!"

Fry had already swallowed his morsel.

Less than 24 hours later, Fry had contracted giardia. He'd eaten squirrel poop. Or fox poop. Or cougar poop. And contracted an awful parasitic infection that entailed vomiting and diarrhea, seriously expensive tests at the new vet, and more days lost to unproductive writing. I carried him down the back stairs a good dozen times a day for him to painfully squirt into the grass as I stood inches away, lest a predator come leaping over the short side of the fence. I had to change something for Fry.

Snow brought the sad solution.

Neither Fry nor I could navigate the back steps any longer in winter. Or should I say 'inclement weather?' Pricilla told me that she'd not taken her heavy winter coats out of storage for more than two years. Kansas City weather had gone wimpy and mild. And yet. Of course. This winter was completely different.

When Meg and her family arrived for Thanksgiving with their sweet white pit bull Rainie in tow, all of us settled in like puppies in a pen. We went up and down the front carpeted indoor stairs visiting with Elvis and Pricilla and her family.

Meg stopped Pricilla and stepped close to her, walking in a circle around her. She held her hands over Pricilla's mid-section and then walked around to Pricilla's back.

"I feel like something is going on in here," Meg said. She has hands that science can't explain. "In there. Do you have any pain?"

Pricilla said no, she didn't.

Meg shrugged. "Ok. Hmm."

Pricilla and her family, and the Nebraska side of my family, all talked about what a strange season it had been over shrimp cocktail and crudités, Brussels sprouts, gravy-laden mashed potatoes and drumsticks. Pumpkin pie and a next-morning bagel spread to beat the band. Quite the strange year weather-wise, everyone agreed.

Fry, we resolved, would need to use the front yard. I would bag his poop every day (even though none of us used the lawn for anything) and he and I would have the security of the front indoor, carpeted staircase to navigate our descent and ascent before and after his outings.

For some reason, Fry didn't really like the freedom. No doubt he didn't like the cold, but something else lingered after the giardia. Maybe he thought the front yard was too exposed, too open. Who knows. I scanned the surrounding terrain like a sniper. I considered carrying my chef's knife outside with me but thought I'd get reported.

"911. What's your emergency?"

"Um, yeah, there's a crazy woman standing with a huge knife in the middle of a front yard. I—I was just jogging past."

So instead I slowly moved in circles, squinting to focus my long-distance vision, sometimes crouching to get a cleaner view of what might lurk beneath shrubbery across the street. I solidified my plan: snatch Fry up off the ground first.

That's as far as I got. I had no idea what I'd do next should a giant fox or cougar appear on top of the neighbor's car. Or on my driveway. It all made me sick to my stomach, each and every outing.

Christmas followed right around the bend. I had to make plans. The past Christmas in St. Louis in the wake of No Joseph

Anymore was hands-down the worst Christmas I'd ever spent, and I was on the path to repeating it if I didn't figure out what Fry and I would be doing for the holiday.

I could have picked Hawaii, but instead I decided it made sense to drive to St. Louis, see family there, then drive to Nebraska and spend the holiday proper at Meg and Lance's. I'd bring Mom for the trip. They had a wood-burning fireplace that roared 24/7. They were nurturing. I felt like the sick girl in junior high recovering from mono. I'd let them take care of me.

In the interim, I tried to write in Kansas City. I added a couple chapters to my novel that had made the finalist shortlist for novel-in-progress in the Faulkner contest. The other submission I entered in the blind-read contest was also a finalist. I had validation that I could still write. I just didn't know how to sit still anymore. I didn't know where to be, in my head, or outside my head.

The end of the first week of December or the start of the second, I'd no doubt started exhibiting symptoms of mental-emotional disintegration. I spent too much time alone. Elvis and Pricilla traveled *a lot*, and while they always invited me down to their place to hang when they were around—quickly wooing Fry with magical dog treats the size of Captain Crunch squares that smelled like liver—I wasn't getting out enough. I hadn't made any new friends. I didn't know how, exactly. My California friend was in California.

I'd tried to go see the Saints play earlier in the season. By myself. In my jersey. Number 9, of course.

Because I am a rabid fan.

The game was in competition with the Chiefs' game that Sunday noon, so it would be a challenge to find it playing onscreen anywhere. I think Elvis had decided that I needed some looking after because he recommended that I head to the

Plaza, the schmancy part of town, to go to a high-end sports-friendly place that wasn't close to a dive. Seemed like good advice.

It took some begging, but I convinced the restaurant manager to put the game on in the corner of the bar while everybody else in the gigantic place indulged in the all-you-can-eat brunch buffet and screamed at the Chiefs. It seemed the very regular Regular, who essentially owned said corner of the bar, had deigned the television channel to be changed for me.

I didn't plunk my ass down and I didn't scream. I gently slipped onto my bar stool and tried to watch quietly, ordering a wine at the bar and later some seafood crudo that happened to be miraculously delicious in land-locked Kansas City. Mr. Regular started chatting me up.

The other bar stools filled up quickly. They'd changed another TV to the Patriots game. We outliers had a small span of neutral zone.

Then a crazy man sat down immediately to my right. I didn't realize something was wrong with him at the outset. People during football season tend to be some measure of inebriated and some level of nuts. But he didn't stop talking, and it seemed he didn't actually realize I was watching the Saints game playing in the corner. I eventually decided, after his repeated visits to the Men's Room, that he was completely whacked out, probably on something much cheaper than cocaine.

Mr. Regular decided I needed rescuing from Crazy Man.

I ordered another wine.

I really just wanted to watch the game. I missed New Orleans and my crew who'd be cheering all together in the same room. Sometimes that same room used to be my living room that I no longer owned.

Mr. Regular started chatting, friendly enough, between plays unfolding on the screens. He was married. Mr. Regular had two young kids. I acknowledged appropriately, telling him I'd newly relocated to Kansas City while I tried to watch Brees and alternately our much improved D.

And then Crazy Man got crazier. The bartender took notice. Mr. Regular said, "Hey, he's nuts." He leaned in. "But he can hear us."

"I know!" I shout-whispered, making a sort of help-me face. A get-me-out-of-this face.

"Text me," he said and gave me his number.

I texted: "Dude is on something."

Mr. Regular texted back.

I texted more.

It took me far too long. I'd not been actively on the market for over 25 years. I hadn't understood what I'd been putting out there, if I had been at all. I naively thought Mr. Regular, with his admission of a wife and two young kids, was just a kind gentleman protecting me from Crazy Man.

He had to repeat the phrase three times before I got it. Before I understood. He texted: "Let's keep it between us. This is just between us."

I texted back that I'd made a mistake and wasn't interesting in what he might be offering.

The Saints lost to the Rams.

And I was an idiot, even more so because I thought I should tell my California friend what had happened. That didn't go well.

But it didn't matter. I'd soon find Moth.

During our 24 years of marriage, Joseph and I had slowly accrued a collection of good art. I don't know if I'd actually impressed upon him the fact that art mattered, considering my background, or if he'd always given a shit about it. He didn't own any art when we met, although that was likely due to the fact that he'd arrived in New Orleans, from suburban Toronto, on a motorcycle.

He did, however, have a strange nearly empty room completely devoid of furniture that he called his study. In it were odd tiny nicknacks and what-nots, tchotchkes. Rocks, a necklace, crystals, figurines, lots of bracelets, all lined up where the wall met the floor on every side of the otherwise empty room. The aesthetic effect was something akin to creepy. Back then he wore a lot of the bracelets, changing them up every few days, tin and silver and brass-turning-green. Those awful black rubber ones that I convinced him to get rid of. These days I suspect the bracelets were gifts from women, but hey, I could be entirely wrong. Maybe he chose all those feminine things that hardly fit his strong wrists of his own accord.

In the last decade, Joseph and I had made friends with artists at Jazz Fest and most every year bought a significant piece or two. Besides the music, the art, to my mind, was the best reason to attend. For a number of consecutive years, we followed the artist Beth Bojarski, whose spectacular paintings we couldn't afford. Finally though, in 2018, she offered a few works within our growing budget. Both Joseph and I were immediately drawn to her painting "Moth Boy." A tight portrait of a boy's face on a moth's body. The painting had a melancholy, *Goodnight, Moon* quality to it, subtle blues and grays. The boy seemed contemplative, wise beyond his years. Beth said that we'd see something else at night if we looked carefully, but she wouldn't tell us what that was. We snatched up the painting before anybody else could.

I saw it first at dusk one evening as I passed "Moth Boy." The boy had disappeared and unfurled his moth wings, right then and there. A diaphanous moth in flight filled the parameters of the boy's visage. Beth had combined the two in the surface image, but somehow underneath, in paint, she had instilled a full metamorphosis from one to the other and back. Or maybe she'd added a layer on top, the glowing iridescent outline of a moth with wings spread. It was magical.

Joseph wasn't around then. Off traveling to spend time with his new child. And his new child's mother. I don't know why I thought that he and I could somehow make a go of it still. I am, in most every way, a fool. But he told me that he'd wanted to fight for me. And I somehow believed him, for yet another little while.

I knew that in the painting, Joseph saw his new son. And I believe he knew that in the painting, I saw a man whom I'd loved so very much but had never acted on that love, not even close. His name was Gord. And he had died recently.

When Joseph returned to New Orleans, I tried to point out the other moth, the true one, in the painting. He didn't see it. "You have to look at it in the right light," I suggested.

I don't know if Joseph ever saw the real moth.

But he got the painting.

I miss it. And I miss Gord. And sometimes, when I can stomach my then ignorance-is-bliss blindness, I miss my old life, the one that I hadn't known was broken even when it was.

The moth, the one I quickly named Moth, appeared just before Christmas. Moth had somehow hitched a ride to Kansas City. Moth had miraculously, unfathomably survived his egg, caterpillar, and pupa stages through countless moves in and out of storage units, in and out of moving trucks, in and out of numerous climate zones and inclement weather. Moth made his appearance in my apartment, in December, in all his huge wing-expanse glory. He batted his way around in the apartment with authority and a measure of undeniable grace. What an extraordinary creature.

So, so out of place. Of course I felt a certain kinship. I'd only seen Moth's breed in New Orleans after a certain point in the year, maybe one or two in our mild winters and early springs. They're rare. Here was this sign, I thought. Here was something I was supposed to pay attention to, even though I was a little scared of Moth. He was big. A really big red-orange fur-collared bug.

And then Moth landed on my lampshade, the silk one topping one of the gray and black lamp bases, and looked like he was settling in for dinner.

I convinced myself I'd had a momentary lapse in judgment. It's just an insect, I told myself. It has nothing to do with any contact from the beyond. You're losing your mind, I told myself. It's a damn bug.

So I captured Moth in a glass and went out the door with him. I let him loose on the concrete floor of my covered second floor balcony. Moth just sat there. I like to think he was smelling the fresh air. Or maybe assessing his new complete freedom. Could he find another breed of moth willing to accept his unfamiliar presence? A new moth partner interested in his flashy, furry collar? I wished Moth luck and headed to bed.

I might have dreamed about Moth. I'm not sure, but he was at the forefront of my mind as soon as I woke up the next day. Fry and I headed out onto the front lawn where I realized immediately it had grown very, very cold overnight. The grass crunched under my bare feet.

Inside and back upstairs, I opened the balcony door and already knew what I would find. There he was, still waiting for his new life to begin, Moth, frozen to the concrete floor.

I felt crushed. Something rattled around inside me. I'd done something cruel and horrible to a small creature.

A piece of my brain had come loose, and it was hanging out with the piece of my heart that had dislodged and gone missing.

I called my California friend and tried to explain my guilt over what I'd done to an insect. I didn't tell him about the painting "Moth Boy." I couldn't bring myself to try to talk about my feelings about a painting as it related to a bug I'd removed from my apartment the night before. I asked my friend if what I remembered was true: can insects reanimate after freezing?

He thought it was possible.

I said I'd talk to him later.

I got a large jar. I went outside and broke a branch off a neighbor's bush. I put the branch in the jar and headed out onto the balcony. I knelt over Moth and gently, as gently as I could, slid a piece of paper under Moth. He looked less than half his size, shrunken in the cold, as if he'd tried to snuggle up tighter against the freezing climate.

I carefully poured frozen Moth off the piece of paper and into my palm and then deposited him on the bottom of the jar. I rubber-banded a piece of wax paper to the top of the jar and poked a few holes in it.

I thought about a short book Joseph had written about a boy freezing to death and what that would have entailed. It was, is, a stunning book.

I went to a noon yoga class in icy Kansas City, but I knew I was losing my grip on reality. Before the final end of Joseph and me, I'd turned to a moth to treat with kindness.

And Moth? In the thawing warmth of my apartment, in his jar with a twig and a couple crispy leaves, Moth came back from the dead. My very own Lazarus. I loved him. I cheered Moth's reanimation. I wish I could have hugged him. Kissed him. At least for a short while, he and I had beaten death.

Christmas arrived. While I was gone, Pricilla would water my plants. My family went through most of the usual motions: baking sweets, cooking the traditional meals, playing games, lots of sitting inside and avoiding the cold. My family knows me better than to have treated me with kid gloves that Christmas, but none of it was easy. I wasn't the only one in our family to miss Joseph's presence. Our nieces and nephews tried to perk up around me, but it had always been Joseph to coax a belly laugh or play the clown, and the kids knew Uncle JoJo would never join us for a holiday again. Not for a snowball fight. Not for a birthday celebration. Not to help paint the ceiling of Mom's back porch. Not to regale Dad with stories of fishing with famous people. Everybody hurt. For a second year in a row. It didn't help that Joseph's new baby had been born on Christmas exactly the year before.

When I drove back into Kansas City on the 28th, my place felt hermetically sealed. What the hell was I doing with my life? Mom and I would stay overnight in my place and the day after next I'd be heading out from St. Louis to California for a short vacation, leaving Fry with Mom once again. I didn't know what I'd be doing in California either, really, but that hardly mattered.

I had barely unpacked my car when a knock sounded on my upstairs, interior door. I opened it to Elvis.

Surprised to see him, especially surprised to see him without Pricilla, I just said hey. Gave him a big hug and asked if he wanted to come in.

Elvis burst into tears. He was back just for a change of clothes.

Wait, what?

Pricilla had emergency surgery on the 26th.

Jesus, what?

In a horrible turn of events, Pricilla's guts had tied themselves in a literal knot. Elvis and she had landed at the ER and after a CT scan, Pricilla was speed-raced away for immediate emergency surgery.

Is she out of the weeds?

Elvis seemed to think that she was but she was very weak, and in a lot of pain. Statistically, forty percent of those with her condition die before they can be treated. She would be in the hospital for many more days. Elvis and she had been planning intensively for nearly a full year for their next photography excursion to India and beyond. No way that could happen now, right?

Elvis shook his head, simply not knowing. They'd removed *fifteen inches* of Pricilla's intestines.

I considered staying in town, but there wasn't much I could do, Elvis said. They just needed to wait and see. I called my sister and told her. "I knew something wasn't right in there," Meg said, reminding me of her magic hand dance around Pricilla's midsection over Thanksgiving.

"It's unreal," I said. "All of it."

So I headed out to California for a visit with my friend and to escape the potential for full-blown depression in a frigid city, my only Kansas City peeps spending their New Year's Eve convalescing. I'd written next to nothing in the last weeks. That's a lie. I don't think I'd written a word. Two novels-in-progress, along with a screenplay-in-progress. Not one word.

After the West Coast visit, I flew back to St. Louis to retrieve Fry from Mom's care, spent a few days, and then drove back to Kansas City when the weather broke long enough for me to not have to tackle I-70 in a blizzard.

Somebody needed to tell me what to do with this wide-open, desolate prairie of future days.

Back and into my 2nd floor duplex tree house, I unpacked once again. Fry seemed happy to recognize his surroundings, rubbing himself on familiar faux fur throws before digging himself a nest and burrowing in for the afternoon. Screw this traveling crap, he said. Screw this pooping in snow thing. My little furry trooper dog had just about given up too, tired of the chaos of the unknown.

Pricilla and Elvis invited me down that evening. Fry perked up some for the visit. They told me that Pricilla's doctor had signed off, and they'd be making their international trip overseas.

"Wow! Really??" It seemed too soon.

"Yeah," Pricilla said. "But Elvis has to deal with this. He has to change my dressing." She lifted her shirt to reveal a still unhealed hole just below her bellybutton in the middle of a long snaking line of brand new bright pink scar. The hole was red, a bit oozy, and stuffed with cotton gauze like a cocktail napkin into an eggshell. "He almost passed out the first couple times he did it. It feels really weird pulling it out."

I looked at Elvis. He clearly didn't relish the thought of performing the task for weeks more.

"I can do it," I said. "It wouldn't bother me."

"It's mushy," I think Elvis said. "And wet."

"I'd be fine," I urged. "Let me know."

"Unless you come with us to South India, he needs to do it." Pricilla's practicality never ceased to impress me, but I worried for the both of them, traveling so soon after major surgery.

Just a few short days later, Elvis had left the building. With Pricilla, of course. They wheeled their luggage down the salt-covered front walkway, hopped in an airport shuttle van, and were gone for the larger part of a month. I'd be plant-sitting.

I thought about how I would make new friends somehow. Someday, I assured myself. In the meantime, I'd go to yoga.

Yoga had saved me before, and it would save me again, I decided. Why not don every warm piece of outdoor clothing I owned, pull on ugly ass Ugg boots, and make a habit of noon yoga? Maybe it would help cure my not-writing.

Less than an hour after Pricilla and Elvis had departed to the airport, Fry started barking at my backdoor and wouldn't stop. I wanted to scold him but then caught sight of the outline of a human being on my rear deck. It startled me. The figure descended the steps.

As the first of a number of very efficient and progressive newly built homes, ours was often used as a petri dish of sorts. Workers came and went in and out of the garage, reading meters, trying new measures to become even more energy-wise, replacing waters heaters with even better ones, tweaking the pumps from the shafts deep below ground.

I often came home from an errand to ladders leaning on the side of the duplex, workers doing something with the solar panels on the roof, so I wasn't completely alarmed about the person who'd stepped away from my back door. Now I heard two men speaking Spanish, which I understand well, to one another on the bamboo-planted side of the building.

I looked out my second story windows on that side of the building to try to see what might be happening next. Were the owners messing with the gutter downspouts or something? I caught a glimpse of somebody wading through the waist-high bamboo. Huh.

I really needed to get in the shower in preparation for yoga, the singular highlight of my day. The Spanish conversation I could discern seemed to revolve around somebody named Victor and Victor's house. Nothing important that I cared about. I walked to my bathroom and took off my clothes, ready to turn on the shower, when one of the voices came back around from the rear of the duplex. Through the fenced yard. Fry barked and barked.

Ok, WTF. I wrapped a towel around myself and raised the blinds on my rear bedroom window. I glanced down to the driveway where the garage met the pavement and saw a worker walking towards the front of the building.

The worker wasn't wearing a jacket. Not even a sweater. He had bare arms. He wore a T.

In January. In Kansas City.

I walked to the front of the duplex and checked to see what truck with some sort of writing on its side was parked there.

Nada. No hay ninguno camión. Nuthin. No truck.

Honestly, I just really, really wanted, needed, to go to yoga, but something was transpiring. I put clothes back on.

I walked from one upstairs window to the next, trying to get a grasp on what the guy was doing. His speaking voice traveled around and around the building. Something, decidedly, was not right.

I grabbed the spare key to Pricilla and Elvis' place. If something bad was happening down there, I should check it out. I was the guardian of their belongings. I should be brave. Because, of course, I'd lost touch with reality.

Key, check. My phone, check. I took a deep breath and headed downstairs, leaving Fry in my apartment. I inserted the key into the Presleys' front interior door and immediately heard clunking metal-on-wood noises. I opened the door wider to see the outline of a person working at trying to force a crow bar—no, wait, it was a giant barbeque tool of Elvis'—into their outdoor balcony door where it met the jamb, the door that led straight into their living room.

"HEY!!!!!" I yelled at the top of my lungs to the person on the other side of the door. "HEY! I'M CALLING THE COPS!!!! STOP RIGHT NOW!!! I'M FUCKING CALLING THE COPS!!!!"

The person didn't stop.

"ALTO!!! ALTO, AHORA!!!" I shouted. "CHINGA TU MADRE!!! ESTOY LLAMANDO LA POLICÍA!!! ALTO!!!"

The person trying to break in still didn't stop. I headed out Elvis and Pricilla's front interior door, locked it behind me, and ran halfway up the stairs. Oh, holy fuck. What was happening?!?

I looked out the clear glass window from the landing and saw the shadow of a man climbing over the shadow of the Presleys' railing that ran around their porch. I watched the shadow man leap off the railing rung and onto the front lawn, a good eight feet below. And there he was in the flesh, the T shirt man again. I assumed my yelling had scared him and that the threat of the police would make him run. He'd take off any second.

Instead, T Shirt Man leapt up onto the main front door concrete stoop and disappeared from my sight again.

I dared descend the stairwell. A backlit dark shadow of a man through the bubbly glass front door tried the doorknob forcefully then shoved his shoulder into the door's wooden edge.

"ALTO!!" I managed one more time. "LLAMANDO LA POLICÍA!!"

I ran up the stairs, locked myself in my apartment, and called 911.

"911, what's your emergency?"

"Somebody's trying to break into my neighbor's place!"

"Your neighbor's house?"

"I live in a duplex. I'm above their place."

The barely muted noises from downstairs continued.

Fry barked his head off, not letting up.

"Ma'am, what is your address?"

I provided it. With speed.

Kansas City is spread out over two states, with State Line Road running through the entire town, north to south. Our duplex was just a block away from State Line. The 911 operator told me she couldn't help me. She was located in Kansas. I was located in Missouri. She'd need to transfer me.

"What?!" How could she be *transferring* me? "I can hear them," I told her. "I saw them out my window. It's the middle of a break-in! *Right now!!*"

"Wait for the next operator," she said and was gone.

I paced my living room. Fry did too, trying to get a read on my face, trying to figure out what was going on.

And then the noises completely stopped. I moved in circles around the interior perimeter of my place, desperate to see something more out one of the windows. If one of the burglars had a gun, he could shoot his way into my apartment quicker than I could figure out a place to hide with Fry.

"911, what's your emergency?"

I repeated myself to the new operator.

How could this possibly be happening in broad daylight? Our neighborhood was safe, supposedly.

I called Elvis who didn't answer. I called Pricilla who did. They were still at the airport, waiting to board their international flight. I explained as succinctly as I could what was transpiring. "Stay on the phone," I told them. "Please."

The cops arrived quickly, multiple cars, without sirens. I opened my balcony door and stepped out into the cold. I shouted over the railing what I'd heard and what the one guy was wearing. They unsnapped their holsters.

A minute later, they walked the jacket-less guy, his hands cuffed behind his back, up the driveway and made him sit on the front walkway. More cops arrived. I went downstairs and opened the front door to talk to two. I held Fry in my sweaty little hands, my phone between my shoulder and ear. I told the cops I'd heard two voices from the bamboo side of the building. They only had one guy so far.

They began a full search of the building. I told the cops I had the tenants from downstairs on the phone. I told the police that my neighbors were on their way to India.

"They're in India?"

"No, they're still at the airport. They haven't left yet."

One cop told another, ""They're going to India." I walked with them into Pricilla and Elvis' place. Their back door hung wide open. The rear window of their home office had been breached, the screen pushed in.

"Pricilla, Elvis," I said into my phone. "They broke into your office." Papers were scattered across large worktables and littered about the floor.

"They're in India," a different cop said to another one. "Two perps, she thinks. Is the suspect out front Indian?"

"No, there were two guys speaking Spanish," I said.

"There were two?" one of them asked.

"I heard two voices," I said.

"Are my printers there?" Elvis, also a photographer, asked on Pricilla's phone.

"Are they missing items?" a cop asked.

"There are two? We have one. Just one." The cops seemed to go on extra high alert.

"There's the big one," Elvis said. "Is my laptop still there? The big computer?"

Fry squirmed in my arms.

"Your laptop is still here," I told Elvis. "What about the garage?" I asked.

"Where's the garage?"

"They're in India," one of the cops said.

Oh no, I thought. The garage doors were always closed, but sometimes Pricilla or I, or one of the workers, forgot to lock the regular non-car door of the garage. There were storage units and utility units opening off the main garage. Oh no.

"This way," I said to one of the cops who'd stuck by me the longest. We went down another set of stairs and I nodded at the closed door leading to the main garage.

Elvis' truck had a winter cap sitting on its hood, and the interior of the cab, full of paperwork, was disheveled.

"Ma'am, ask them if he left a hat on the truck."

"What's behind those doors?"

"Those are storage units. And utility closets."

A cop tried Pricilla's and Elvis' storage unit. The door was locked. I opened mine a tiny bit and stepped away. A cop stepped up and flung my door open.

"Ask if they locked their storage unit." The cops clearly didn't like the garage. They didn't like the balaklava on the hood of the truck.

"Elvis. Did you guys actually lock your storage unit?" They never did, far as I'd known.

"No, I don't think so," Elvis said.

I shook my head at the cops and inched away.

They drew their guns with a precision and speed I'd not anticipated and aimed them at Pricilla and Elvis' storage unit door. "POLICE!! COME OUT WITH YOUR HANDS UP!!"

"COME OUT NOW WITH YOUR HANDS UP!!!"

"Oh my god, oh my god," I half whispered to Elvis and slunk backwards towards the interior door to the stairway. No gunshots came, but I didn't know where to stand.

I walked up to street level where more cops had appeared, one clearly in charge of the handcuffed man sitting in just his T shirt on the freezing walkway. I felt pity for him. It couldn't have been more than 25 degrees out.

T Shirt Man, upon processing the fact that I was scared, holding a chihuahua, talking into a phone, cops guarding me and asking me questions—his face changed completely, and out came a steady stream of broken English. He was so sorry, a mistake. He made a mistake. Victor told him to break into his house.

"Victor?" I asked. "Victor no vive aquí, y tú conoces! Donde?! Donde esta Victor? Dime! Mentiroso!"

We continued in Spanish. Victor was at work. Victor told T Shirt Man to break in.

"This isn't Victor's house. There's no Victor here and I think you know it. Where's your jacket?"

He didn't have a jacket because he'd been in jail the night before. He called Victor with his one phone call. Victor was at work.

"If you know Victor, why were you trying to break into a house that wasn't Victor's?" I wanted to get to the bottom of the absurdity.

Wrong address. I'm sorry. Victor lives down the street.

"Wait, so *you know* where Victor lives?! Where's the other man? Who is the other man?"

There's no other man. Just Victor.

"Victor?" a police officer asked. "Who's Victor?"

"They're in India," another cop said.

"Garage is clear."

I looked the man sitting on the walkway in the eyes and realized he wasn't completely lucid. I swear he sent a little kiss to Fry in my arms. I swear his heart melted just a tiny bit in this freezing city for my tiny fawn chihuahua. I worried I might pass out. I'd done that once before in the Houston airport.

"Hey, Amanda?" Elvis asked.

"Oh, shit, hey, Elvis."

"Can you take photos of the office and send them to me so we can do inventory?"

"I need to take photos of the office," I told a cop. "For the tenants."

"Of course. They can file a report. We'll leave the form."

"Says they're in India," a nearby cop told another new one on the scene.

T Shirt Man, well, evidently he'd been working solo. He indeed had been in jail the night before. He'd been talking to Victor as he circled our duplex, speaking loudly, Victor on speaker. Or maybe to just himself out loud as if to Victor. But if Victor had actually been on the other end of a phone, possibly a burner phone, T Shirt Man had ditched it. The Kansas City police department deported T Shirt Man a few days later. I thought about how cold he'd been sitting on the walkway. And I wondered, just a little bit, if there could have been a bit of truth to his story. It's possible, isn't it? I wanted to believe it.

He'd stolen nothing from Pricilla and Elvis. He'd broken into their apartment through their rear, unlocked window after dragging a patio chair to reach it. Because he needed to find a place to lay his head, to finally sleep. But after he'd gotten in and saw Pricilla and Elvis' artwork and unfamiliar surroundings, he'd realized he'd broken into the wrong house. He'd quickly exited their backdoor and hidden under the rear stairs, where the cops found him. He'd just wanted to sleep. After a night in jail. In someplace warm.

It's what I choose to think.

———

A couple weeks later, after I'd spent countless hours attempting to find a proper writing window of time that never materialized, after I'd harvested every last seed from my dozen jumbo pomegranates that I'd purchased at Costco, after I'd made batches of chili and vacuumed the crap out of my apartment, after I'd become a yoga zealot, shopped online for new outdoor coats and boots, waited for Pricilla and Elvis to return from India and take me someplace interesting to meet interesting people, I started having nightmares.

Three nights in a row, I jolted awake at the exact same time. Each night, I'd had the same dream. An enormous creature with talons the size of paring knives swooped into the yard, snatched up Fry, and flew off with him while Fry made the most horrible, plaintive, panicked screams I'd ever heard. Fry. In my dreaming mind, he was gone and would be eviscerated alive in his painful final minutes.

My heart thunked in my chest. I woke myself up with my own jerks and muffled half-screams, my face wet with tears and sweat.

The first night, I chalked it up to my brain doing its housecleaning thing. Processing horrors. My recent life horrors.

The second night, I took note of the time on my phone. Three o'clock in the morning. Exact same time. Jesus. Something, somebody, might be trying to reach me.

The third night, upon waking, I could barely swallow. What were the chances that this would happen at the exact same minute, the exact same dream, for a third time? My panic, the trauma, my sorrow for the dreamed experience wouldn't abate. I lay in bed and cried.

Fry has always slept in my bed. In the first weeks after Joseph and I rescued him from Florida, he'd burrow his way down to my feet and lie somewhere around my calves or ankles. I worried he'd suffocate so far under the covers. Eventually he made his way up towards the pillows. He curled himself, when he could, into my abdomen, his nose a few inches away from the top of the sheet. I sleep in a C, sometimes an L. He'd found his sweet spot.

That third night, I tried to control my sobs. I petted Fry and told him I loved him and that I would do everything possible to keep him from harm. Somehow he's always understood what tears mean. He scootched out from under the covers and licked my face.

After a few more fitful hours of half-sleep, I rose from bed the next morning, feeling nothing more than dread. Fry had to go outside. The rear stairs were iced over, of course, and we'd have to go out front as was the norm now. I'd have to watch for cougars and foxes, and an infiltration of coyotes that had recently been reported on the news.

Fry's complete rejection of a leash and collar or a leash and harness had me trying to figure out a way for him to relieve himself and not freeze to death. We'd kinda settled on my walking a couple feet behind him and scoping the horizon.

And I know. I'm aware. It was a terrible solution.

With the dream still fresh in my mind, I acted as Fry's sentinel, holding the plastic grocery bag I would use to pick up his poop as he made his mincing way across the frozen but bare front lawn. My caramel-colored dog with monster ears and a white fur bib nearly matched the color of the winter grass. I know I should have had 100% concentration on him. I thought I did. I scanned the near and far around me. Fry took a few more steps forward while I remained vigilant.

The thing, it came in silently.

Right then, a huge ferruginous hawk or juvenile eagle, with a wing-span as large as my own, swooped in over my right shoulder. I never heard it. Not a prayer of my having heard it.

It came in and dove at Fry, its talons and legs extended, wings fully engaged. I saw the little furry feathers on its haunches. I saw everything: this extraordinary predatory creature in mid-capture of its meal. The moment happened in slow motion. Nanoseconds ticked past.

The talons were as big as my own fingers.

My nightmare. My nightmare. My nightmare.

It stalled for a wing beat in the air, stopping its forward momentum, less than a foot above Fry's back. Going for the plunge, for the snatch of its prey off the grass. I whipped the plastic poop bag overhead and screamed. And by the grace of some intervening soul, the bird of prey decided I posed too much of a threat. Or that's what I like to think. I like to think I saved Fry.

The hawks, and the eagles, are indeed bigger in Kansas City.

I watched the bird of prey fly up to the high branches of a neighbor's tree. It sat and watched as I kept it in my vision while Fry pooped, completely unaware. I can only thank a higher power for that, too. Had Fry ever grown conscious of a threat from the skies, we'd have been completely and utterly doomed.

From that moment onward, Fry adhered to my leash policy. He hated it, but it didn't matter. I told him that I wouldn't let him be snatched from the ground. I wouldn't let him be flown off into the skies. I needed to preserve the one and only entity that I'd retained from my marriage that mattered at all.

For a short while, I turned into the woman who needed to be reported.

"911, what's your emergency?"

"There's a woman holding a dog on a leash in her front yard."

"Sir?"

"I'm pretty sure she's not well?"

"This is an emergency line."

"She's, um, she's waving a wooden thing over her head. I think it's a police stick. A, uh, a billy club. And she's staring up at the sky. She just keeps waving it in circles over her head."

"Do you feel she is in danger? Is she going to harm herself?"

"Ah, I couldn't say."

———

By mid-February, I'd given up my billy club routine although I'd gotten quite good at it. I thought of the club as my adult baton. I considered throwing and catching it but worried my doing so would scare Fry. Besides, just getting Fry outside took too much energy.

———

March either arrived like a lion or a lamb. Whichever, it wasn't memorable. Beyond Pricilla and Elvis, I'd made no new friends. My niece lived in town, but she was a fulltime student busy with her own life. My California friend and I had broken up and then decided to give it another try, but things with him never really meshed in a cohesive way again. All the teachers at noon yoga knew me, and some of the other regular students and I were chatty, but nobody asked me to do anything with them. I wouldn't have known what to do unless a neon sign flashed: FUN. MUSIC. DANCING. FOR PEOPLE YOUR AGE WHO STILL WANT TO FEEL RELEVANT. DON'T BE AFRAID. COME THIS WAY.

A few art openings. A gathering at a restaurant with Pricilla, Elvis, and some of their already attached friends. Small, short opportunities. I added hummingbird tattoos to my forearms. I developed a crush on a guy at yoga. Much to my amazement, it seemed mutual. I had to make one last trip to New Orleans, at the start of April, and then I vowed I'd be brave enough to ask out handsome Yoga William.

I bought a red flowered dress for my April trip. Because my lawyer said I should be there. It had a low-cut V neck, delicate sleeves, a fitted waist. Mom would watch Fry at her place in St. Louis, and I'd fly down and back from there.

In New Orleans, I parked my rental car in a parking garage across the way from City Hall. A block-wide park abuts the monolithic, architecturally drab building. There's a small stage-gazebo there in the park and crisscrossing concrete walking paths. Usually homeless people I try to treat with courtesy. I'd spent countless hours at City Hall the past number of years getting permits for home renovations and going to hearings about the proposed plan for the abandoned school building across the street from my home.

To say I felt out of my body isn't exactly accurate, but I felt very much, well, in the moment but not fully in my head. It felt surreal. I walked across the park in my pretty red dress hugging a manila folder of paperwork. My heeled pink suede shoes with open toes, red trim, and ankle straps were just a little too big.

They slipped some, and I remember thinking with each stride closer to City Hall, that I was taking historic steps. I was doing this thing. This thing I could never have imagined.

I will never forget being sworn in. And I will never forget that I was the only one of us to appear. I didn't know it at the time, but a month earlier Joseph had his second child with baby mama. Guess he couldn't make the trip down. I don't know.

Looking around the courtroom, waiting for my name to be called, I considered the other women there. Some surely wanted what they were about to receive. Others, not so much. Me? I heard Colin Hay in my head. I tried fiercely to stay conscious, to not faint. I managed it.

On April 3rd, 2019, I walked away from the building with signed copies of the divorce decree. I wondered how many other women in America had walked my same footsteps, across a cobbled lane, a rutted road, a busy intersection, over a hill, a bridge, an industrial canal, down a meadow path, through a parking lot. I did not feel special. I just felt different.

In our first months of graduate school, in the fiction writing section of the Creative Writing Workshop at UNO, Joseph and I soon learned we had very different writing practices. I'm an obsessive editor. I might get a full page of text out, maybe, before I double-back and reread. Make it better. Get it cleaner, tighter. Joseph was always the opposite. He let everything pour out before he revisited. He kept moving forward. I turned around, always, to look back from where I'd come.

Over the years of our marriage, I kept up my editing habit, both with my work and with Joseph's. We were each other's first readers. Always.

Walking, after my divorce, across the sorry-looking park outside of City Hall, speckled with homeless people and the lumpy piles of their grand sum totals of earthly belongings, something came to mind. I tried to figure out what I was feeling.

I hadn't cried, and I didn't think I'd need to the remainder of the day. After the courtroom though, my adrenaline buoyancy, a helium balloon losing height, just drifted down to the earth. Right there in that dilapidated green space surrounded by tall downtown buildings, the April sun hot on the top of my head, I recalled an early piece Joseph had written in grad school decades ago. The piece revisited a single word far too many times, one I'd pointed out in my margin and line notes to him so long ago, but, in the moment of my walking away with the end of my marriage, I might have finally understood the true sentiment behind it: melancholy.

I flew back to St. Louis and then drove to Kansas City once more. I found very little humor, or delight, in my life, but I was, am, a trooper. What more was there to do than to persevere? I don't know that I'd ever felt so emotionally flat. Handsome William, why, oh why, did you never return to noon yoga again? I swear I was going to ask you out.

Spring crept in around the edges. Crocuses poked out of the wet ground and took a look around. Daffodils followed suit.

My writing went nowhere. Elvis and Pricilla went everywhere. They traveled constantly. But they always invited me down to hang out when they were home. We drank wine and ate nuts and talked about the world.

In early April, Pricilla smacked her head on her kitchen counter late at night while fainting. She'd gone to get a glass of water. It happened again a day later. Elvis caught her the second time. Something wasn't right. Off to the hospital they went.

After EKGs and many tests, Pricilla needed to have an ICM, an insertable cardiac monitor, implanted in her chest.

Unbeknownst to her till that week, she'd inherited a genetic anomaly that could kill her as quickly as a proverbial widow-maker could a man. She would be convalescing for many more weeks. She couldn't go to her favorite boxing workouts. She couldn't drive. The ICM needed to record her heart first so that doctors could determine whether she was fit for strenuous activity down the road. Down the hill. Down the lane.

My old footsteps weren't materializing in Kansas City. I'd had a vibrant, boisterous life as an undergrad student there, but I couldn't figure out a way to reconstruct it. And Pricilla, generous, kind, funny, half broke-down Pricilla, couldn't drag me around as she tried to heal for a second time in nearly as many months.

I checked the horizon every day, for hawks and something, anything, Fry always on his leash.

How does a human being, who'd planned on getting old with the love of her life, sitting on a porch swing at the end of their days, how does that human start over? I have no children. I am no longer young.

I needed love, and my family gave me all they could manage. I can't really blame my German heritage. 23 and Me has told me I'm more French than German. Lots of Scandinavian and a smattering of other things in there too. But our family isn't particularly demonstrative. Nobody's fault.

Others in New Orleans, friends so close that I consider them family, started texting from afar. "What are you doing there?"

"Just come home," they'd say.

Honestly, I had no idea. It just wasn't turning out all that well. I needed more support. I needed people who'd already had my back for a quarter century, ones I could see every day if I wanted. The ones whose doors I could knock on with no notice and they'd welcome me in, give me some pickled green beans or marcona almonds, a stiff drink or a soft shoulder, and talk me down from my own personal cliff.

My niece in Kansas City had an end-of-semester show—she, too, is an incredible artist—and Pricilla began to heal, preparing for her own massive photography show. Me? I decided I would start packing. Again. I was moving back to New Orleans.

The boxing, the wrapping, the padding, the taping, the planning. All of it, all over again. My third major move in under eleven months.

Things are just things. But they can conjure memories. They serve as tactile sparks from the past. Outside, on my block in Kansas City, the green leaves spread their fingers, and the squirrels living in the tree out front had babies. The squirrel toddlers made short forays out onto fat branches before they chickened out and dove back into their hole. Kansas City was hatching the season I'd missed. Having arrived in October, I'd miss summer again.

I took down my framed set list of the Tragically Hip's final show, one of many shows of theirs that I'd been unbelievably lucky enough not just to attend and hang around backstage but to write about in Maclean's. I swathed my weighty stone Buddha in a moving blanket. Grandma's china got boxed once more. But over my months in town, in small invisible increments, I'd come to realize I didn't need everything, all that stuff from the division of moveables, every last scrap of nothing-special anymore. I could manage with less. I could maybe, possibly, be happy with less.

A few days before loading up Pods in the driveway, I had a garage sale. It wasn't particularly successful, but I don't miss anything that I sold, and I donated the rest. Some years back I'd read about the practice of the Swedish Death Cleanse. The gist is that we opt to live our lives as though we might die later that day. That we leave in our homes only what would be easy for family members to clean up and sell or distribute amongst themselves or to outsiders. We're also supposed to keep our psychic rooms just as clean. No bulging closets. Nothing left unattended-to. No regrets over things left undone. Look around your place before you depart for the day, and what would anybody find in the wake of You No More?

She drank a green tea. She made the bed. Her laundry was in the hamper. Her closet was orderly, although her jewelry was a bit tangled.

So here now in New Orleans, I've been working towards a true Swedish Death Cleanse. I'm closest to full success in my tidy library-study where I write. The books are organized on tall shelves. There's a pleasing symmetry to the room, a small round table, balance, a lack of visual clutter. Sometimes I listen to Arcade Fire because their songs make me smile. The music will always remind me of the time Joseph and I, along with seven or eight visiting friends, were invited to wear huge papier-mache bobble heads on stage at Jazz Fest and dance with Arcade Fire for their opening number. In front of tens of thousands in the audience. Joseph and I had become friends with some of the members of the band. That's how it went in those days, those magical days before the fall.

My giant bobble head was Bono's. A 6'5" friend's head was Obama's. Others were the band members' heads themselves in detailed, hyperbolic, overdrive. We had to see out through mouths that were covered in mesh, or through tiny eyeholes that didn't exactly match up with our own eyes. Electrical cords snaked in and around the band's equipment. But we took to our roles with abandon. I didn't care if I face-planted front and center, crashing in slo-mo, on repeat, on the big screens on either side of the stage. None of us did. We paraded and strutted and danced our asses off, our hearts on fire with the beautiful absurdity, the joy, the joy, of it all.

I have nothing physical from the experience, just the memories. I hope maybe some of the friends still have a couple photos at least. And I hope they look back fondly on Joseph and me, the two of us still a singular entity then. In my calm library-study now, with my snoring chihuahua, I remember that day with a full heart.

———

After Moth came back to life, I had to decide what to do with him. To release him outside would surely freeze him again, likely into oblivion after more ensuing months of snow. I researched, and what I found wasn't promising. The sole purpose of a moth's last stage as an adult is to procreate. They don't eat. The males only mate before they die.

I had a magical creature from the Deep South in a jar in my Kansas City apartment in the middle of winter. He batted his wings again and again against the sides of the large clear jar. Beautiful as any butterfly I'd ever seen. I had no idea what to do.

The exterior hallway was three stories high with large, unopenable windows. Moth could fly around in the stairwell, I decided. It was warm enough to keep him alive. He would never find a partner. Although he'd never eat much again, I set out a small bowl of sweetened water, like nectar, if he got thirsty.

So I did that. Because I had sympathy for an insect. Because I was trying to be a decent human being in the wake of a wide-open road of pain.

My friend Moth flew around a little in the stairwell for a couple days, but it was really just a bigger jar. Usually when

I saw him, he was trying to get out through one of the panes of thick glass that would never have opened. The last day as I passed by, he landed on my arm and wouldn't get off.

He had bashed his head into the glass long enough. It was time.

"Ok, sweetie," I told Moth. "Well, then, let's go."

I carried Moth down on my arm and rather than going to my car in the garage, I opened the front door. The morning snow had melted. The temperature was above freezing. Moth didn't want to leave my arm, but I had nothing more to offer. I scooped Moth gently off my jacket sleeve, crouched, and placed him on the grass. Thank you, I told him, for your beauty. His bright orange-red furry collar glinted in the sun. Thank you, I said, with all the sincerity I had in this world, thank you for your company.

And then I left.

———

Carly Simon has a book out about her friendship with Jackie Kennedy. Recently I drove to yoga and listened to an NPR piece on it. Such a wonderful friendship. How different the two women were. Jackie admitted to Carly that yes, of course she knew about Jack's affairs. But that ultimately it was ok. Because Jack loved Jackie so, so much more than all the rest, she said. She knew it. I pray that Jackie's assuredness comes some night to me as I dream, a small miracle, when the moon is full.

———

Pricilla said I needed to go with her to see an art installation before I left Kansas City. I didn't have too much left to do at that point. The attempted transplanting of this New Orleanian hadn't really stuck, obviously, but I would retain plenty from the effort. I'd seen the toddler squirrels turn into juveniles and head out on their own, brazen as human teenagers. I'd helped my niece move a number of times and had the opportunity to see her grow as an artist. I'd visited with so many family members, more than I had in years. It wasn't all a wash. Fry had survived lions and tigers and bears, cougars and coyotes and hawks, giardia and snow and ice. He tore off a dew claw and needed minor surgery, but he survived that too. I'd managed to survive the lesser but obvious challenges. At the end of the day, I'd somehow retained my sanity. I chalked it up to the very notion of transition. It's never supposed to be a permanent state of being.

Pricilla took me downtown to a giant wind art installation. I'd seen videos of it, art constantly being on Kansas City's radar, but it was impossible to capture the beauty of the thing on late night local news.

Pricilla and I lay on the grass beneath it and watched. Listened. Stayed exactly in the moment. It spanned nearly an entire downtown city block. Rigged between buildings from overhead, made of crisscrossed and interwoven wires, every inch knotted with long silvery, rustling strips of light-catching mylar cellophane, the installation shimmered and breathed. It wasn't a grid, although the smallest sections of it were neatly woven. The wind caught it and it rose in undulating waves. It was a lung and a bird wing and an ocean and a whisper, grace incarnate.

I contemplate the lessons I was supposed to learn from my time revisiting the Midwest. In my wildest writer dreams, I consider it my chrysalis stage. I am different, this side of it all. Certainly

Pricilla is different too. Did some higher power throw daggers at her, at me, at Fry, and dare us to dodge, to adapt? Did we finally get to the end of the gauntlet? Could this finally be done, at least for now? I walked the lane. I slew the dragon. And I got the dog. Fry with his wonky, foggy left eye. His howls as I ascend my apartment stairs. His scarred apple head, his scarred belly. His joyful racing when given a free expanse of space, as though he will burst if he can't run at maximum speed. His snores. His yawns. His foot chewing and his sneezes. I got the dog.

How did you get in here? How did you manage to make it into my life without my knowing? What could he have possibly told you to have you believe that I was a non-entity?

Glitz. Glamour. The peak of it all. What a ride that must have been.

But it's not cool to entrap somebody by telling him that you can't get pregnant.

Maybe, though, that was his idea, what you two decided you should tell me.

Interloper

So. Yeah. I sit at a few different places in my apartment depending on the task at hand. In the early mornings, I edit first thing, straight away. Later in the morning, I sit in the bigger area of my apartment, the whole thing open to the rest of everything else—the TV remote hanging out with the giant clamshell filled with onions on the kitchen counter, the folded laundry on the living room chair. I sit on a tall chair at a tall table to answer emails, pay bills, avoid Facebook, and generally impose structure on my mid-mornings after Fry has been fed and the real world outside my interior parameters has materialized into something via The New York Times. In the afternoons and evenings, I reserve my study-library for Writing-writing.

I need to say this. I do. I am not making up what is about to come.

So, yeah, one day, mid-morning, I'm sitting on my tall chair at my counter-height table and I'm just slowly moving my gaze around the main room of my apartment. I like visual inspiration, but I don't really need that right now in the moment, massaging my foot arches on the chair rung, since I'm not doing much of anything. My Zillow habit of searching for homes I can't afford has been a lovely fantasy distraction of late. Oh, look at the place over on Willow. Sweet house on N. White.

Like I said I'm sitting there, facing the window that offers a view of the backsides of neighbors' single-story homes. The houses' butts. Usually my blinds are closed just enough that sunlight strikes my cup of tea beside me but I don't have to contemplate the butts if I don't want to.

Looking, looking, just around. I lean forward to crack my back with an arch and. Huh. What is that?

Fry doesn't have toys. He doesn't know how to play with them. Some people find that fact super sad. Me? I think he thinks it's kinda dumb, the playing with toys thing. Right after his adoption, he'd fixate on soft squeaky toys but only to eviscerate them, pull out the stuffing flesh, remove the squeaky plastic heart, chew a hole in it, and then be done with it. He'd stopped the noise. That was his mission. He accomplished it and gone back to doing his other thing: guarding me.

What am I looking at? In the corner, a giant glazed ceramic planter, nearly four feet tall, contains mother-in-law plants. You know, the wicked tongues. Abuse them and they only get stronger.

Something is sitting on the corner of the Persian rug, tucked in behind the giant pot. Even though Fry doesn't have any toys, my automatic first thought is that the thing is a dog's toy, tossed and ignored. But I know it's not. The apartment building hasn't had any pest issues. I doubt it's a mouse, but damn if it isn't about the size of a dead mouse. Wouldn't Fry bark at a mouse? What *is* that?!

I'm not a chicken-shit woman. I've stomped on roaches with bare feet. I've inserted myself into the middle of physical altercations between humans. But sometimes, especially in the mornings when I'm only partially aware, I don't necessarily lead off my daily routine by being brave. I look again down the expanse of wall and behind the giant, really really heavy pot, and consider what's there. Hmm. I don't like it.

It's going to have to be a hands-and-knees kind of thing. Because, of course, I'm the only one here. My life's in shambles and this is just part and parcel. If anything else is going to go wrong, might as well be now.

So I crawl, on my hands and knees, towards the thing by the bottom of the planter.

Are you kidding me?!

It's a mushroom. A now completely dehydrated and collapsed mushroom. Even in its current state, it's *still* as big as a dead mouse. It must have been as big as my hand when fresh. Alive. And it grew out of the *bottom* of the giant pot.

Oh, no.

That means at one point there's been moisture there. And spores. Sitting on my 11' x 14' hand-woven rug. I thought that the three feet of bubble wrap at the bottom of the pot would have stopped any leaking when I watered the plants on top, but I now realize how foolish I'd been to think so.

I get up off my hands and knees, retrieve a paper towel, and then head back to pluck the mushroom out from under the foot of the pot. The mushroom disintegrates to powder in my hand and it occurs to me that it could be poisonous. Great. I've just released a plume of poisonous mushroom spores into my living room. I hold my breath and walk the paper towel with the crumbled mushroom to the garbage can and throw it away.

It's up to me to see how this thing happened to grow here. To see what's under the pot now. So much for heading to noon yoga.

The pot weighs over a hundred pounds. It's as wide as a barrel-chested man. I remove three tubs of mother-in-law. The bubble wrap smells musty, but it's not wet.

I can lift and hold the pot for maybe five seconds at a time. It's awkward. Slippery. It doesn't have handles. It's not malleable like a real live barrel-chested man. I'll need to move the furniture so that I can lay the planter on its side—assuming I can get it to the ground without dropping it—and then roll it away to deal with the rug damage. Surely for a mushroom to grow from the bottom of the pot, or from the rug itself, there is damage.

My sister Meg and her husband Lance have been married since she was 20. She wasn't even legally old enough to drink at her own wedding. She did anyway though, because that's Meg. Sometime over the course of their now 33-year marriage, Lance (who has a incorrigible sense of humor and little patience for a disorderly house) coined the term 'dick job.' They'd been mildly arguing about chores. Meg hadn't wanted to do something, and Lance said, "Oh, I get it. That's a dick job." Their bickering nickname stuck, and that's how they divide all the laborious tasks. Dick jobs, and non-dick jobs. Most often the dick jobs involve machinery—they have a lot of land, a tractor, a snowplow. Oil changes. Chopping wood for the fireplace. Some of the grosser household tasks, dealing with recycling, taking out sloppy garbage bags. Anything involving heavy lifting in their house, though, is a communal chore. Because it's hard to lift things alone.

Joseph and I never adopted the term, but we thought it was funny, and the division of our household chores also fell into more or less the same sort of categories. I cooked but then Joseph did the dishes. He dealt with our Jeep. I dealt with paperwork. As our marriage progressed in years—is that an accurate way to put that?—and as Joseph began to find reasons to be away more often than he was home, I literally took on the bulk of the heavy lifting in our house. I learned how to move furniture by myself. They make wonderful slippy-disc things that, if you can lift the corner of the sofa long enough and slide one of the things under the leg with your foot and repeat three times more, you can push a huge couch around by yourself. Make sure to get both kinds: one for hardwood and one for rugs and carpets.

So. Back to the mushroom. I no longer have a partner. But I have a dick job that needs to get done. I've got all eight slippy-discs. I lift the sofa in increments then push it out of the way. Next the coffee table. After that the two matching side chairs and the heavy swiveling chair.

I can't ignore the heavy pot any longer.

Fry has grown to despise change in his household. Any. Something gets moved, pulled off a shelf, rearranged or tidied, even if I'm just doing laundry, he interprets it as impending change. Three major moves in 11 months can do that to a dog, I guess. I feel him.

And yeah, so Fry has long retreated to my study while I work towards getting to the root of the mushroom. Just as well. I don't want him inhaling any spores.

I step up to the giant pot and tip it towards me, checking out the weight. I feel sure I can at least lower it successfully to the floor, which is what I do. I glance quickly at the rug after I've tipped the pot on its side. Oh, man.

Black mold.

I awkwardly roll the giant planter away and return to the scene of the crime. I'm looking at road kill. I stare at the perfectly round patch of completely ruined carpet and wonder what I can do to salvage it, if anything. Mold, in New Orleans, is a death knell.

I can't pour bleach directly on the rug. But I do have the can of natural disinfectant from Whole Foods. It says it kills over 99% of the bad pathogens and all the other things that need killing. I need to use that, at least. I go get the spray out from under the kitchen sink and head to the black round circle on my rug. I unleash a dick job's worth of a motherlode spray onto the circle.

OK. So that should be it, right? But the black mold stays black. And I'm dumb worried about the hardwood floor beneath the rug.

I look around as though somebody else is standing nearby, as though somebody else who's seeing this will respond to me and say, "Whoa." Somebody who will say, "Hey, get out of the way. I got this."

Do it, girlfriend. You can do it. Deal with this situation. Because you can. You're able-bodied. Not one other soul is going to come to your rescue right now.

I pull back the rug corner and look at the spot on the floor.

It's not nearly as bad as I expected. I can contain the damage, sand it after the circle of wet wood dries and rematch the stain. After all, the building has withstood rain through broken windows for over a decade, post Katrina. I can do this.

For some reason I think to look at the underside of the rug corner that I still hold in my left hand. Because I'm left-handed. Which means that the whole world is aligned against me. Although it's not the world's fault.

I drop the rug, and it falls neatly into place again.

OMFG.

What is that?

I know I don't have any construction dust masks left. I used them all up in my moves.

Despite my instinct to heed all better inclinations, my curiosity kicks in.

I need to see.

I pull back the rug corner yet again.

And then I pull it farther.

The black circle, sprayed from above with the disinfectant, has completely fallen through. It has turned to mush.

But on the underside of the carpet, a web of white fungus is spread like something from a horror movie. It's huge, as wide in diameter as I am tall.

Towards the center it looks like white asparagus.

At its tender webbed fingerlings, it's thin as spaghetti.

This thing. This thing has been growing under my rug, in my living room, under my radar. What. The. Fuck. Is. This. Thing.

I pull the rug even farther back.

I want to throw up.

In the moment I know I will drag this beautiful rug out to the dumpster. And in the moment I know I will have to conquer this insane infiltrator. This is mine alone to slay.

I get the spray once more and let the huge circle of whatever it is, the interloper, have it.

If I can impose a soundtrack, it squeals. It doesn't squeal, but in a movie, it would have.

The thing, the giant circle of a thing, it moves. *IT MOVES.*

I spray it with repeated rounds of disinfecting spray, and it starts to shrink up like an octopus withdrawing. Oh, holy everything that is holy, I don't know what to do with this thing.

I stand over it, the can of spray in hand, and I have a rare flash of objectivity. I am battling fungus, or something else of an organic nature, that has overtaken my rug. I am battling much more than that, I know, but in the moment, I am going to destroy this mo-fo. I am getting rid of this beast.

And so I do that. I drag all the furniture off any bit of the rug and then begin the taxing process of getting the rug out of the apartment. I put on rubber gloves. I have to get it out.

By the time I'm done, I've lost four hours to the mushroom project. I've lost a beautiful rug. I assume that most people dragging dead bodies are too consumed with their task to notice how hard it is to actually do. I don't have a literal dead body in hand, but the rug is heavy as any dead body ever.

I finally manage to get it out into the hall, and I send it careening down the back hall stairs. Good riddance. It slumps, getting caught up halfway down the steps. Of course. Because this is my life.

Gotta tug. Gotta sweat. Gotta work at this. Because.

Just because. That's how it's gonna go.

Sometimes, close to the end of us, Joseph couldn't keep his stories straight. He went to Toronto for meetings and then forgot what he'd told me. No, he hadn't met with his editor yet. Yes, he'd met with his publicist for lunch. He was going to go over to Gord's and see him.

The next day it was all jumbled. No, he still had to go to lunch. He was going to see his editor again even though he'd said he'd seen her the day before. No, Gord was tomorrow. In my gut now, I know where Joseph had been. With Her. Lunch, dinner, overnight to breakfast and over again.

Now, at this distance, I look back with wonder at what fire Gord brought to call attention to First Nations struggles at the end of his days. Yes, Joseph had carried kindling. But so many other First Nations advocates had been shouting from the tops of pyre stacks for decades. Centuries.

It is a sad fact that we globally still largely listen to white people. I hate it. And I'm white. But Gord? He loaded that fire up with hardwood for First Nations support and set it ablaze. I hope it roars forever.

Dragons

Gord Downie and I were dear friends. In the year after his diagnosis of terminal brain cancer and surgery, he asked me to write him 43 poems before he died. He told me to hurry. He never told me the significance of the number, but I suspect I know the meaning. When he was still healthy, we'd been in Woody Point, Newfoundland vacationing together with his family, Joseph, Shelagh Rogers and others, and we'd talked about the Chinese zodiac. Ended up Gord and I were both dragons.

Love Letter to a Dragon #10

Orange-furred dragons feast in Australia,
fox-faced bats eating fermented fruit.
They fall from trees, take drunken flights as
awe flutters into my earthbound heart.

Bryan, one of the richest dudes at our admittedly privileged St. Louis high school, summered in California because his family had places there, too. Plural.

A wide-eyed, open-minded teen, I decided to take the Greyhound bus from St. Louis out to San Diego. Because my parents let me. And because I wanted to.

Bryan's mom was sleeping with a guy in my high school class. Because she wanted to. And because she could. Out in the California summer, she tended her La Jolla garden in a bikini top, and her chosen boy toy, my classmate with a buzz-topped mullet a la Ziggy Stardust, walked around in a Speedo, his notable endowment on unavoidable display. I learned what Dom Pérignon was. I learned what cocaine was. I learned how to be gracefully nonchalant on giant sectional sofas, how to not eat very much, and how to watch the show of real life with a pretend jaded eye. My guy then was into punk rock, sang in a band, got rip-roaringly drunk and did things like borrow one of the numerous Vespas that Bryan's family had in the garage, drive around the coast in the middle of the night, wreck it, and land his ass in the hospital.

I don't know how many true friends Bryan had then. He was the beyond rich kid with the messed-up parents, his father absent, his mother an emotional child. One of Bryan's superficial St. Louis friends stole one of Bryan's many guitars but then felt guilty about it. The guy returned the guitar to Bryan, pretending he'd apprehended it from another guy who'd been the real one to take it. It must have been a moral conundrum though for the thieving friend. When somebody has a ridiculous amount of everything, of guitars and Vespas, houses and cars and bottles of champagne and drugs, would one guitar even be missed?

Our high school wasn't that big, but it was, and remains, a behemoth in its reputation. The likes of Andy Cohen have come out of it. Celebrities, uncountable scholars. It's a fancypants place, known in the entirety of St. Louis for being a rich kids school. A lot of my classmates lived in large, stately homes, some true mansions. My friend Lynne had something like 19 bedrooms in her house, the third story having been designed originally for 'the help.' Bryan lived on the same looped road, all the homes modeled after British country estates. Bryan sometimes wore a top hat as a kid. He was dropped off every morning to grade school in a Silver Cloud Rolls Royce.

My parents managed to get us girls into the school district by the tiniest of margins, buying a house just three away from the St. Louis City border. We had three small bedrooms and one and a half bathrooms. Our house looked nothing like Bryan's, but I still had free access to kids like Bryan and the uncontained chaos of his multiple homes.

I don't think it's fair to say that Bryan was lonely, but he carried with him a quiet pensiveness that always surprised me, a smooth stone he fingered in his jacket pocket. In the middle of some massive, debauched gathering that had been extended for days on end, his whole house a crash pad for homeless kids and kids who could get away with not coming home for days, for users and punks and hangers-on, in the middle of the smoky haze, floors awash with empty bottles, staggering couples heading up the stairs to use somebody's bedroom, there Bryan would be, staring off into the distance, sitting calmly in the epicenter of a world not of his own design.

After high school, I never spent any time with Bryan again. But recently a mutual friend told me.

Bryan died of a heart attack this year.

Love Letter to a Dragon #25

ink inside skin
to mark the days
and breaths
of sweetest air
so much oxygen
beside a tannin tea
of river
to remember
our blue heart clan
and sink after sink of dishes
wet hands fires dogs
noise of engines
family rain
boots and hearts and so much
mud so much
slippery life

Glenn, Lance's dad, might as well have come straight out of *Gunsmoke* or *True Grit*. When I first met Glenn, he was a cattle trader with multiple dusty pens of bovines on the edge of Fremont. He also owned the adjacent Western wear shop. Glenn wore cowboy boots, and sold cowboy boots, and generally exuded all things cowboy boots. Meg and Lance and I, in college together, made a road trip from Kansas City to Nebraska for Thanksgiving.

I'd been intimidated, for some reason, to visit Nebraska. It felt raw to me, as though a whole other way of life, the rules of which hadn't been revealed to me, sat there out on the plains. How would I know what to do? What if I made an idiot of myself because I didn't understand what to say or how to be? Lance had grown up riding bulls. He and his dad were the real deal.

Glenn wore Western wear shirts with pearl snap buttons, his hard belly contained by a leather belt with an ornamental buckle. He loved to talk. He drank coffee throughout the day and flirted with everyone, his employees, Meg, women in their 80s, me. If Lance hadn't forewarned me about Glenn's ridiculous party trick, I might have been horrified.

In his shop, Glenn went behind the cash register counter and pulled out a walking cane, handing it to me. "Hold it in both hands," he said about the cane. "What do you think?"

I thought it wasn't a particularly good-looking cane.

"What do you think it's made of?" Glenn asked. He was going to get the city girl, but good.

I wouldn't let him have it though. He had placed a shellacked bull dick cane in my hands. "Biggest penis I've ever held," I said.

Glenn laughed and laughed, tickled pink by my flat delivery. I'm sure I'd been blushing nonetheless. I'd also bet real money that no matter what the woman on the receiving end of the cane said, he laughed and enjoyed himself plenty, each and every time.

Meg and Lance married in Nebraska, and Glenn and I saw each other many times over the next decades. He liked to gamble in casinos. He ate steak at his favorite steak houses, dated a woman named Emma Jean, drove luxury sedans, and finally, in his last years, the cattle-trading done, the Western wear shop sold, he chose to care for the infirmed elderly for extra money.

It seemed like such an odd option to me. He changed bedding and bathed people. He often had to feed them. He had been so social, and here he was, helping other humans in their ultimate months, people who remained silent in the presence of his small talk. He poured himself a coffee and sat down to chat, one-way. I think about that tender gift he offered them. I think about how he'd likely hoped somebody would do the same for him.

I'm glad Meg and Lance were able to be there for him in his final days. He died last year.

———

Love Letter to a Dragon #30

Thank you
for our life

It crept on cat feet
beneath our seats
up our thighs and
over our asses
stood our neck hair on end
gave us shivers in the thick
heat of your concert

the thing
the combustible thing
the ridiculous fusion
love sound abandon
made us remember
our first bike rides
no training wheels

Lisa and I thought we were tied for the worst last name in junior high, mine unpronounceable on sight, hers auditory-odd. She kept hers over the years while I shed mine to take on something a phone solicitor could actually manage. I've only recently learned how the kids you knew when you were young normalized your name straight away in their own heads. That's just who you were, what you were called. Oh, that's Banana Cankles. She's on the dance squad. Laddie Vucksiss, damn, he bit it at the finish line of the 800 meter dash.

I borrowed pieces of Lisa's life and fictionalized them for *Pretty Little Dirty*. She had an enviable family, boisterous and arty, a father who couldn't be more of a presence if he'd tried. He encouraged young women to speak their minds, to read the newspaper every day, and to enjoy their food at the dinner table. They lived in a cool condominium like New Yorkers. When I went for sleepovers, Lisa made us sophisticated snacks—garbanzo beans swimming in balsamic, stovetop popcorn sprinkled with Parmesan and paprika. She spoke French and studied modern dance at the university level.

In high school, Lisa traveled to France for a year abroad, and while she was gone, I grew nine inches in nine months. I was a homely late bloomer when Lisa initially befriended me. Upon her return, she simply couldn't believe how I'd matured. She said so repeatedly as we sat on a friend's living room floor at a New Year's Eve party. After she came home, Lisa and I remained familiar, but I zigged one way with friends while she zagged the other.

Some years later, Lisa and I landed in a number of the same modern dance classes at Washington University in St.

Louis. The dance professors singled Lisa out time and again for dancing a sequence perfectly, for dancing with her heart. It was something I didn't yet understand how to do—how to imbue your art with heart. To make matters worse, I had a crush on one of our teachers, a handsome Asian dance professor who smoked cigarettes in the campus café while I lurked nearby with my bagel, trying to look all casual, all cool girl about town. I don't think he recognized me out of the context of the dance studio. He read a book and ignored me. And then in swept international Lisa, a gorgeous scarf around her neck, a great European bag slung over a shoulder, and suddenly who stubs out his cigarette, stands, and greets her warmly? Who suddenly wants to talk? He knew exactly who his star pupil was, Lisa of the long neck, Lisa who understood what the French names of our dance moves actually meant. She owned encounters like those, could order a tea and sit down with a professor or other students and talk like an adult about adult things. I could do nothing of the sort, but I so desperately wanted to be just like her. I wanted to somehow replicate her grace.

A few years ago, Lisa put the word out to friends. She was sick.

The gift of time to say goodbye to somebody you have loved, you still love, is so much truly that: a gift. It hurts. You gotta be brave. But it is so worth it.

Lisa and I caught up in St. Louis. She'd made the trip from out East with her husband and teenage daughter. I'd made the trip up to St. Louis from New Orleans specifically to see Lisa. A few other friends came in from elsewhere for Lisa. She was showing her daughter and husband where she'd grown up, revisiting her childhood. Here is where I lived with Grandma and your Grandpa when he was still alive. There used to be a hairdressing shop in that building. Here is my junior high. This is the park where I rode my bike. It's a seven-mile path. We'll go to the Art Museum later.

Lisa said she wanted me to herself for a few hours, so her husband and daughter did their own thing while Lisa and I met at an Indian restaurant for lunch. She sat across the table from me and smiled. She'd given up on pretending about her hair and sported a fluffy halo of sorts. We laughed about our last names, about all the nicknames we'd come up with for ourselves. We talked about dancing and about our careers. She said she hoped to make it to her daughter's high school graduation. That was her goal. Then we headed back into our communal youth. She needed to remind me once more of how she couldn't get over how I'd changed the year she'd been in France.

"Oh, you were something," she said. "I mean, you, back then, wow. Just wow." She glanced away, seeing 35 years into the past.

I started crying. How could she have the wherewithal to compliment the high school Amanda when she was so sick? Her grace, all of it, was still so intact. She gave it to me in those few hours with her full heart.

She died of brain cancer, like Gord, within months of him, in 2017.

Love Letter to a Dragon, #17

the skies are full of birds
and you seed the air
let us feed feed
flutter gorge
no way to say thank you

but to show up again
again again
we are here

———

Julia, Joseph's sister, stood for me beside my own two sisters the day I married Joseph. Six months pregnant at our wedding, Julia wore a floral dress and held a colorful bouquet over her bump, watching her baby bro do the biggest thing of his life thus far, in America, under a giant live oak tree in a park in New Orleans. She smiled with her eyes always, and that's what she's doing in our wedding photos.

Julia was buxom and never afraid to highlight her assets. After we'd met for the first time, when Joseph and I had just started dating and had made an incredibly long road trip from New Orleans to Toronto, Julia told me at the breakfast table that she slept in a bra. She had to keep the goods protected. Then she pricked my finger with a needle from her diabetes kit. She said I had borderline low blood sugar.

Like more than half the Boyden children, she'd been an untamed teen. She challenged her mother's patience by dating Jamaican guys she met at the Younge Street restaurant where she worked late at night. She opted to stay blonde while her siblings' hair darkened. As a young adult, she worked with disabled children. She helped them glue things on paper, took them sledding, put on tuques and removed tuques, put on mittens and pulled lost ones from mountains of snow. Arranged snacks. Laughed and excelled at her job.

She met the love of her life, and they had two sons.

I could never figure out the reason, but Julia's house was always on high volume, everyone shouting normal sentences. Julia's laugh was even louder. It's legendary in certain parts of suburban Toronto. If you stepped foot out of your car and could hear Julia's laugh inside the home, you knew the party had started. Julia didn't drink much but was so happy to be around happy people. Her enthusiasm infected the entire scene. She carried trays of appetizers at other people's houses. An entertaining unicorn, she refreshed beverages and introduced people, making connections for the shy ones, listening to the boisterous ones with patience. By Julia's book, adults needed candy, too, at Halloween, and every inch of every room had to be decorated at Christmas.

She had a soft spot for underdogs. Joseph's firstborn son, over the years, had grown into a teen with odd habits and temperamental outbursts. A great kid, I thought, whom I'd gotten along with since he'd been in diapers. But nonetheless a vexing one. He'd started testing the boundary waters. Joseph and I offered to take him, in New Orleans, but that didn't go over well with his mom. Nobody could deal with him regularly. Except Julia.

After her own sons had grown, Julia returned to caregiving work. She was too good not to.

At one of Joseph's last Toronto book launches, at a chi-chi gathering in a rented-out restaurant on the near West side thrown by his longtime editor and the publishing house, most all of the immediate Boyden clan who could attend, did.

My friend April and her husband had made the flight up, all the way from New Orleans. April and I had purchased party dresses and packed heels in our suitcases, but both of us had not understood the climate differential. The heat of the crowd warmed our arms, at least a little. There would be a few short speeches. And there would be music. One of the people who'd be singing some songs was Gord Downie. Because he believed in Joseph. Because he loved him.

After people talked and gave thanks to the writing and publishing entities, Gord began his short set. I stood by Joseph, April and her husband nearby. The gift of Gord's presence astounded me. The crowd hushed in respectful awe. He sang, and while he sang, in the background, somebody's voice broke through. Somebody was having a loud conversation while Gord sang.

"Oh my god," Joseph whispered at my side. "Somebody make Julia be quiet."

Julia talked and talked. While Gord sang.

It ended up that Julia had been trying to help a disabled cousin in a wheelchair get a better view of Gord on the impromptu stage.

That's who she was.

Julia, my bridesmaid I loved beyond measure, died of a blood clot to her heart this last year.

———

Love Letter to a Dragon, #19

in a small and ragged bar in Santa Fe
a live band played surrounded by World War
memorabilia dirty people dirty tables
strange sculptures swimming on the ceiling
and I thought of you, thought of dancing
realized I've spent so many years not
so I stood and left my seat, the others
and danced till sweat rolled down my spine
it felt so good I could have screamed
I know I know I know exactly what you mean

Little boy Franz arrived in America in 1921. He was left-handed, not a sin in Germany, but as a young kid in Minnesota he was forced to write with his right hand, his left tied behind his back. He was forever after ambidextrous, not a terrible trait.

He said his family had been long suffering in Germany, where Franz had contracted TB. When he was five, he'd been sent to a Catholic sanatorium in the Swiss Alps to recover for over three months and became fixated on cod liver oil. The nun nurses had to hide the bottle from him because he craved it.

Over eight decades later Franz wrote, with his left or right hand I can't say, "When I was about 5 ½ years my mother said I snored so they sent me to a doctor to open my nostrils. He had me kneel on a stool, hold a stainless bowl under my chin and proceeded to crack my nose bone. I knelt on that stool for what I thought was a long time and I had to go to the bathroom. I was afraid to tell him for fear that the doctor didn't want to stop. I peed my pants."

Franz became Frank in America. His young boy body responded to adequate nutrition, to pork chops and fresh apples, whatever else Minnesota dished up. His parents planted a garden.

He loved the local pool as a child, excelled at swimming and diving, and in school learned his second language quickly. He loved mathematics. He embodied pretty much every last stereotype a blue-eyed, blond-haired immigrant German kid could have in the '20s. He went nuts for his little family dog, a curly black-haired cocker spaniel with a white-tipped tail. Frank taught Tip to follow him off the high dive.

Years later, Frank met a raven-haired beauty, Deloris, and they married with next to no time to spare before he was deployed to the Pacific in the Navy in WWII. While Deloris gestated my mother in her belly, still smoking—because nobody knew any better then—Frank fought in Eniwetok and Kwajalein, among many others, working as an engineer on the mammoth ships as well as driving landing boats. He dove deep, deep underwater once, in his most famous anecdote of bravery, to disentangle a giant chain anchor line caught on something. He succeeded in freeing it, under enemy fire, and helped save the ship.

Frank, an exceedingly clever man by any measure, had aspirations after the war. Mom was joined by a younger sister Cheri, and Frank went into engineering. Deloris sewed and baked, tended house, doted on their kids, and Frank joined the semi-secret forces of the Honeywell corporation, working on parts for the military, parts for civilian security, and multiple other parts for other half hush-hush projects.

In his spare time, Grandpa Frank took up woodworking and filled his garage with an array of high-end power woodworking equipment. Whenever we grandkids went up to Minnesota, Grandpa had a new project. He built a gazebo. He framed out and tiled a spa tub for Deloris. He built a giant addition to their house. Boom. The man was able.

Frank didn't get along with our father, and Dad didn't like Frank. But Frank looked damn good in his tight-fitting clothes into his 90s. He did push-ups everyday. Joseph used to say that Grandpa Franz—he'd returned to his authentic name at some point in his later years—beat Joseph hands-down in a wife-beater contest. After Deloris died, in her mid-70s, Franz dated plenty, exactly the way Deloris had always said, with rue, that he would do.

A number of us in the family pestered Grandpa Franz to write down his memories of the war. I have two of his spiral notebooks, his cursive precise and distinct, the ink color changing with the entry dates. Describing a rare down-time day, his German-Minnesotan accent, I think, is audible:

"I had a bright idea + told my buddy Marv in the engine room that we should invite the executive officer. He was pleased and went to the Pharmacist mate + obtained 2 pints of Overland whiskey. The exec was a mustang and so was the cook, they both came up through the ranks. Every time the cook went ashore, he'd come back to the ship with another tattoo.

"The following morning, the one Higgins boat was lowered, we all climbed aboard. The gunnery officer was the chaperone, the cook had buns, wieners, pickles, you name it. We also had a volleyball. The exec took off bars on the beach and said 'You guys can treat me as an apprentice seaman.' I made him a drink and said, 'Here you go, you S O B.'"

When younger and throughout the war, Grandpa Franz was a gymnast. I inherited the penchant. My sister has a photo of Grandpa, on a horizontal bar on one of his Navy ships, doing an inverted plank, a move that requires an amazing amount of strength. It's an elite move. Franz decided to just, oh, hang out on the ship and exercise a little. And hold himself, from a ship pipe, in an inverted plank. A fellow Navy man snapped the shutter on the camera, had the film processed and then printed after they'd left the war, and sent the black and white photo to Franz. We have the image now.

For many years, Grandpa Franz and I were the only ones in our family with tattoos. He got a kick out of the fact. His, a Navy anchor on his inner forearm, spoke to who he was. He touched the hummingbird on my right wrist and said, "They sting a little, don't they?"

As the years passed, Grandpa Franz's energy didn't abate. He didn't stop moving, and man, did he love to dance. And dance. At my second cousin's wedding in the early '80s, when I was 18,

Grandpa Franz swung me around, dancing the polka for hours while all the rest of the guests blurred into the background. He led me across the floor, pushed and pulled me the way I needed to be guided. I twirled and laughed, screwed up. He set me straight again and corrected my missteps. I'd never had so much fun out on a dance floor. I've yet to dance with a better partner.

Franz died, at 96. At his funeral, a lone bugler played Taps.

Love Letter to a Dragon, #9

he was raised by wolves my husband their exhausted mother her litter eight too tired to descend the basement steps to stop the growling too tired to notice the snakes or believe the pain inflicted by the alpha surely too tired to know how they fed themselves bathed slept curled or flat piled when each day she left to fend for them all she alone

he laughs at what he thinks is my joke about his youth my husband the sound of it romantic maybe shared meat and so much fur strength and abandon guardians at his back but I have never told him that I know they had to nuzzle together their own world push sticks into piles stones and patch with pack loyalty gallons of blood broken bones

he somehow does not know his own bravery now innate when he howls across the plains of snow and wheat and through the trees to call the other lost ones or when he says he would surely tomorrow give his life for yours

dear dragon he does not know how few would trade
make the leap lunge at the cavern and scream I will do
this yes

———

Joseph and I met Gord Downie in person, the very first time,
together, at Gord's house. His (and his family's) address was
not regularly divulged. Gord had a stalker, and then some.
Joseph and I arrived in the morning and Gord brought us into
his kitchen, the counter covered in the dregs of multiple kids'
breakfast, cereal bowls, juice glasses. He asked if we'd like
anything. Joseph and I declined and attempted some state of
cool, but it wasn't going to work. We were visiting with Gord
Fucking Downie. I asked about the pets and expressed interest in
the art I could see from that vantage point. Eventually we three
sat outside at a little table on his lawn. His wife, significantly
pregnant at the time, walked past on her way to yoga in her
leggings, her face a singularly beautiful smile. She welcomed us
and headed out.

I looked at the exterior of their house where a ladder
reached to near the roofline. What were they having done? Gord
shared a story about a rogue raccoon in their attic that they'd
tried to capture that very morning. Gord seemed begrudgingly
accepting of the wild animal's attempt at finding a perfectly
protected haven.

We became friends.

Years later, I mailed Gord's youngest, the baby bump that
first day who'd grown into a fabulous boy, via snail mail, a secret
clue detective letter that I'd handwritten. He needed to figure
out how to read it in the mirror, with a key. Gord helped him
decipher it.

Gord died on October 17, 2017.

Love Letter to a Dragon, #32

me: So if you could be an animal, what would you be?
You: I'd be a human. A father. A writer. And a damn fine dancer.
me: I think animals dance. Sometimes. That's kinda lame. I'm just trying to connect. These poems are really hard to write. I don't know what to say sometimes.
You: Pretend each day counts.
me: I try that. I really do. Sometimes it works, but not always. [Pause.] I would be a bird. Or maybe a large cat.
You: Why?
me: Of course you'd just ask why. Maybe I'd like to be a redwood tree.
You: Why?
me: Because I've been thinking a lot about not being me. I'm a slow learner.
You: We all are.
me: You're just trying to make me feel better. What year were you born? I know the answer already, actually. I'm leading you. Can we decide that you'd be a dragon?
You: Sure. If you want.
me: I'm a dragon too. It's the one connection I've clung to. Like a starfish at low tide. I don't know. That's lame too. [Pause.] I could try to find you. After.
You: Sure. If you want.
me: I can't do this. Actually, I don't know how to do this. Thank you for being so nice.
You: How about a starfish?
me: Or a star? A sun. You're a sun, for sure.

You: What did they call those things you could buy in the back of a magazine? They were human seahorses. Families of seahorses.

me: Yes. They were called something! Whatever they were. How many of us tiny human seahorses could be in a family?

You: As many as you want.

me: Ok. I want a lot. Like a ton a lot.

You: Me too.

me: We can eat seaweed. It's really good for you. [Pause.] I love you. For seaweed and stars and birds forever.

You: It's ok. It's all ok.

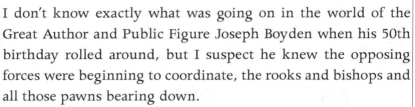

I don't know exactly what was going on in the world of the Great Author and Public Figure Joseph Boyden when his 50th birthday rolled around, but I suspect he knew the opposing forces were beginning to coordinate, the rooks and bishops and all those pawns bearing down.

For months our sister-in-law had planned a surprise birthday party for Joseph at their beautiful lakeside home with over fifty guests. I flew up from New Orleans to Toronto, and Joseph flew in from a long haul away. When we found each other finally in the airport, he'd had a meltdown. He stood with his forehead against a huge glass pane and wouldn't move. I don't know what was on the front end of that meltdown, but I had pity for him. I saw the boy in the man.

When he finally did speak, he said he'd made a reservation at a Toronto hotel for us that night. I didn't understand. He knew we were due to be up north in a matter of hours in a rental car. Why wouldn't he explain his headspace? I had to tell him about the surprise party. People had driven and flown in from all over. No, no, no, he said. He didn't want a party. I said it was too late not to have one. I called our sister-in-law, and she found a nephew to pick us up from the airport and make the three plus hour drive north. Joseph slept the whole way.

That day, I think, Joseph had seen it all through to the checkmate. He'd finally gotten trapped in the corner of no escape, the king trudging one square by one square till the bitter end. It still makes me sad.

Second Chance

A guy in Texas, Ralph Fisher, in the early aughts, decided to clone his Brahman bull. While driving on my way to buy groceries—in New Orleans we say 'make groceries' sometimes—I listened to an NPR interview with Ralph. His first bull, named Chance, clearly had been unique and much loved. When I tuned in, the cloned bull named Second Chance had been assessed by Ralph as nearly 95% of the original Chance. Then Second Chance gored Ralph. The *second* time Second Chance gored Ralph, the bull did it in front of the producer of the program. Ralph ended up with over 80 stitches, many in his scrotum.

A year and a half later, the production crew revisited Ralph and Second Chance. Second Chance had mellowed into a better approximation of the first Chance. Ralph just said that, in essence, he'd been keepin' on keepin' on with Second Chance. Bringing him feed and giving Second Chance a life. He adored the bull. Gorings can just happen.

He overcame it eventually, but Dad caught pneumonia when I was in fourth grade. Mom didn't actually believe Dad had been particularly sick, so Dad had to call his parents to come get him and take him to the hospital. Mom had started working as a waitress to help pay bills. Maybe she was too distracted to see Dad's symptoms clearly. I don't know.

With Mom working and Dad in the hospital, we three girls needed some semblance of care. The eldest, I still wasn't quite old enough to babysit. Somehow or other, through some strange connection via Grandpa's church, we ended up with a caregiver. I'll call her Eunice.

Eunice was elderly, significantly so, in the way in the 1970s that made you think she was ancient. She was a spinster, and overweight. She wore no makeup, and she didn't smile. Not at all. I wondered if she had teeth, since she never showed them. When she spoke, it was in heavily accented, stilted English. I'm going to bet, considering that Eunice was Lutheran, that she was German.

Eunice was missing a whole hand.

We girls hadn't had a lot of exposure to people missing parts of themselves yet, so Eunice's wrist stump was pretty fascinating for us, never mind the fact that we suddenly had complete free reign of the townhouse. I didn't think Eunice was able-bodied enough to chase us upstairs, but Eunice could tell on us to our parents. How well would we actually have to behave? Oh, the conundrum.

Mom was the cook in our house, and she usually opted for her traditional family recipes. Chops. Kraut. Potatoes. Massive amounts of other vegetables. They were cheaper than proteins.

Whatever sacrificed animal it had come from, the roast was formidable. Mom couldn't have known it would prove difficult for Eunice. I believe Mom thought she was treating both Eunice and us girls to something special.

Eunice didn't ask for help. She managed to get the roast out of the roasting pan and onto some platter or cutting board without any assistance.

At the dinner table, she looked at our fascination, our stares, and went at it. She held the roast with her stump while she carved with a huge knife in her remaining hand. I know it's unkind, but the stump was the perfect approximation, the way I remember it, of the end of a turkey leg. Only a little bigger. Her flesh-covered stump. All three of us girls stared. Young Emily's mouth hung open. I thought that maybe Eunice should have a strap-on specialized prosthetic that she could use with different utensils she could fix into the end. She could have a giant fork. She could have a hammer and a screwdriver. A hairbrush. A big carved tobacco pipe like Grandpa's. Or a fake hand she could cover with a leather glove. I decided she should wear an eye patch too. And tall black boots.

None of us could eat much of the roast except Eunice. We'd lost our appetites. As soon as we were excused, we raced upstairs to our bedrooms. As I'd suspected, Eunice didn't follow us up. She managed to do the dishes one-handedly and settled in on the sofa to await the return of our mother.

If I could dial back the clock and return to 4th grade, I'd ask Eunice what happened to her hand. Scars crisscrossed the end of the stump and ran partially up her forearm, so she'd likely actually *had* a hand. Had she worked on a farm in Germany as a girl and lost it in a mechanical accident? Had she been fighting on the wrong side of the war and a French soldier had shot it? How often did Eunice return to the moment when she lost her hand and wish she'd had a second chance to redo the one thing that led her to losing it? Might she have had a husband except for her missing hand? Could she have had better jobs, not have to take crappy babysitting gigs and rely on the kindness of the church, if she'd had two good hands? I don't know.

What if we all had only one second chance to do one singular thing over again? And that thing could turn out the same, better, or even worse. How many people would take the chance, knowing that they had just one-in-three odds of a more positive outcome? John could try again to play in the NFL. Laura could apply one more time to med school. Rico could make mac-n-cheese and try not to fall asleep again and not burn down the house.

Sometimes we actually do get second chances in real life. Not many true ones, but we do.

———

I decided to jump out of a plane, the first time, in California. I'd moved to L.A. temporarily to work for a friend from Toronto who'd opened up her first talent agency in the states. Joseph was gone, up north, and I thought L.A. could be a great opportunity to expand my horizons. I'd spent time out there, a lot of time, when I was younger. I liked L.A. I saw it for what it was, a more laid-back and much friendlier city than others deduced from a distance. The West side, especially, had a vibe that I appreciated.

On my days off, I'd take the bus from North Hollywood to the beach in Santa Monica. I brought my trapeze with me, its heavy hockey-tape wrapped bar and velvet covered lines familiar as a long-loved bicycle for someone else. I hung it on the beach from one of the super tall adult swing sets rising up out of the sand. I climbed up to the top bar and rigged from above, trained as long as I could in the sun, eventually unlocked the carabiners, unchained it, and took it back home on the bus.

One of the days, the surf quiet and nearly flat, rollerbladers passing on the boardwalk, somebody approached me, a cool Cali chick kind of girl. "Hey, alright, yeah. You go! Nice one. What's that called again, a fallen angel?" She had lanky long blonde hair and freckles, and like me, wore leggings.

I smiled upside-down and did a monkey roll so I could sit on my bar for a second and talk. "Yeah," I said. "Hey."

She introduced herself. She asked if I tumbled at all or did hand balancing. I said I did. She told me if I wanted to come jump after I was done, she was pretty sure I'd be accepted into the club. The trampoline club. A stuntman, a little person stuntman, owned a trampoline he'd pull out of a garage right there on the boardwalk next to a café, and then he and others would set it up out on the sand. A half dozen people whom he approved of bounced till they tired. I'd been hungering for time on a trampoline again.

Cali Chick introduced me to the others. They needed to see if I could pass the test, whatever exactly that was I'm not sure. I got up and did some consecutive front and back flips then a couple full twisting layouts, and the little person owner nodded and gave me a thumbs-up. I was in. One of the other jumpers was spectacular. Double-twisting double-backs. A triple tuck. Seemed his real passion, however, was jumping out of planes. He just practiced on the tramp so he could duplicate it in the air with a parachute strapped to his back. That, and he was a professional stuntman. Most all of them in that crew made their money doing stunts. I'd found my peeps. I'd found a secret clan of Grandpa Franz's offspring right there, under my nose, in Santa Monica.

I started training stunts with a number of the crew, and one woman and I became good friends. She had access to a retired stuntman's backyard flying trapeze rig. Only if stealing jewels had been involved could I have been happier.

I flew. I jumped. I trained trapeze. I got lunch for my boss. I ate all her spicy pickled carrots and jalapenos out of her part of the to-go order from the local taqueria before I handed it over to her. I entered data on her Apple computer and let my wavy hair grow out.

After maybe a month, the guy who was so good on the trampoline asked me if I wanted to go jump out of a plane. I said I couldn't afford it. But he'd just passed his next-to-last level towards earning his master jumper certificate and he had a free guest pass. Yes, he was trying to woo me, even though I'd repeatedly told him I was married, but I'd get to *jump out of a plane for free*. I didn't blink. Yes, I told him.

He picked me up very, very early in the morning, and he and I drove out to the desert. Perris, to be precise.

I've never been much of a morning person, and this one was painful with a virtual stranger, heading out to the middle of nowhere, trying to make small talk in a small car. I remember nothing much more about the drive than that it was boring and that I wasn't sure how smart the dude was. I have a few biases, the need for intelligence being one of them. But for this opportunity, I'd have made a drive twice as long.

The stunt dude joined his other peeps, the ones with many many jumps under their belts, while I went through the rigmarole and hoops. I was forced to watch a video that essentially said, over and over, you are signing your life away. You cannot sue us. You are taking this upon yourself. Do you understand what it means to jump out of a plane?

Then came the actual practical bit. The desert was hot. Those of us first-timers were given a talking-to. In really hot full body jumpsuits. Pay attention to what your jump guide will be shouting in your ear. Pay attention to everything. Pay attention to your altimeter. This is how you will be strapped together. You will be the one to see the ground easily while your jump guide will be strapped to your back. You will share a chute. It will hold you both. Come here. Step close. There, yes, here is how you will be attached to this other person. Otherwise you can't free fall. If you don't want to free fall, you can opt for another half day of video and classroom lessons, and then you will be allowed to jump by yourself while your chute deploys the instant you leave the plane.

Hellz no, sister! I want to free fall! I'm so stoked I can taste it. I am going to do this, and I am going to get to be the bird I've wanted to be my whole life.

I end up with a Vietnam vet pro jumper wearing a spandex get-up with shorts. He'll be strapped to my back. I can't feel more comfortable, more secure. He cracks jokes, which I assume is de rigueur for newbies. We pile in the plane, all of us first-timers glancing around.

I don't know what I expected the interior of the plane to be, but it's not this. It's just one big wraparound slippery aluminum bench. It's weird being harnessed to a stranger, a dude with his front half pressed to my back half, but hey, I'm going to fly.

We've been instructed that when the time comes, when we've hit the designated altitude of a bit over 10,000 feet, we will be given the go-ahead from the pilot, and off we will scootch, down the aluminum bench, two by two, and out we'll leap into the air with time enough in between each pair. Remember not to make shapes other than relaxed arms and legs extended. We won't be trying to dive, not this time. We will reach our terminal velocity in this shape at 120 miles per hour. It will be very hard to hear. Descending at this MPH is loud, mo-fo loud.

The interior of the plane is dumb loud already. We make big graceful loops in the plane ascending and ascending like a turkey vulture in reverse. On the other side of the aluminum seat, a couple of the people pinned to the fronts of the jump pros don't look so hot. They look like they might throw up. They look like they might poop their jumpsuits. Me? I'm giddy. I've wanted to do this my whole life.

My Vietnam vet pro yells in my ear, reminding me about the altitude to pull the ripcord for our chute. He gets us ready and scootches us down the aluminum bench. The pilot gives the signal. We're not the first to go. We are maybe fourth or fifth.

On our turn, we hold ourselves in the open door. There's a count: 3, 2, 1, JUMP!

We go. I hold my body the way I was instructed. The hot air feels like it suspends us, and I am flying.

I am flying, and the earth, from this height, is art, and everything is hot desert air, noise, face-down immediacy, beauty. I am a grinning fool. I am a bird. For at least a few minutes. I can't believe what is happening in so many ways, but I am so present. Inside my goggles, I can't blink.

Other jumpers who went before us begin deploying their chutes in the distance, and I look at our altimeter. Floating down will be fine, but the speed rush of free fall is my jam.

Time to pull the cord. My pro gives the thumbs-up.

I yank with a good tug, and just like in the movies, the chute comes out of the pack that my pro is wearing and we jerk up with a lot of force. We catch a different kind of air, slower, and align ourselves vertically to the earth for the first time.

Oh, here comes the drifty, easy, slow part. We're falling waaaaaaay slower, and then, suddenly, we're not.

My pro is jerking behind me, lurching into my back. We're plummeting almost as quickly as before. I don't understand.

I think to look up. My guide's tugging on the guy lines on the big chute. It's tangled itself into a parachute blob, and it's losing air. He's trying to disentangle it.

The lumpy chute collapses like a dying jellyfish, tucks itself into the rest of the failing entity, and twists up into a hard knot. We are freefalling fully, completely, again.

My dude, my Vietnam vet, has to do something. He'll do something, right?

Oh, god, I've always known that I'd go in some strange way, but the very first time I jump out of a plane? Really? Really?

Is this going to hurt, hitting the ground at this speed? Or will I just black out on impact?

Look at all those other jumpers, floating slowly to the ground. Over there in the distance. We're not anywhere near them anymore.

My pro wriggles behind me as though our lives depend on it, and they do. He's trying to get rid of the failed chute.

And I think, Well, it could be a bit of a cushion. Should we really get rid of it?

He finally succeeds in releasing the useless lump. I keep watching the ground coming closer. I think about what I still want to do in my life.

It's so loud. The wind blankets what is about to happen. I will die in the desert. I will smash and bounce, attached to a stranger, and I will never again see the earth from above.

He does something, and suddenly we catch air again.

OH. MY. GOD. The ground isn't barreling up at us at even half the speed. What has happened? I look up. There's another smaller chute deployed over our heads.

I'm not going to die?

Maybe I might not die?

He taps me with force on my shoulder. "See that tilled-up circle over there?!?!?!" he shouts in my ear.

He points, not an easy thing to do, and says, "We're aiming for that dirt circle!!!"

The air in my ears is still so loud I can hardly hear a thing.

"Have you ever seen any World War Two movies?!?!?" he screams.

"Yes!!!!!!" I holler.

Something isn't right with the chute we have now. It doesn't seem to have any directional ability, and we're flip-flopping all over the place like a seed pod from a tree.

"We're going to aim for that!!!" he yells.

"OKAY!!!!!" I respond.

The ground gets closer. I guess tilled soil might be softer.

The earth isn't quite as pretty at this distance. Or it might actually be prettier. Right now I am thinking about how I will be meeting it. I am trying to process if these images will be the last I see.

Soil. Scrubby brush. Plow lines.

"We are going to have to roll!!!" he screams. "Really roll hard, like in World War Two movies!!!!!!"

I show him a thumbs-up. What else can I do? We are careening, maybe, hopefully, towards the circle of tilled dirt, flopping, a kite missing the tail.

Look. There are birds down there, pecking food out of the fields.

"If I yell LEFT," he hollers, "we have to go that way! I won't know till we get there! Don't GO RIGHT if I say LEFT!!!!!!"

"I GOT IT!!" I scream back.

"It might have to be RIGHT!!!!"

"OK!!!!!" I shout. We're bobbling as though in a dingy on horrible surf. Here comes the ground.

We swing wildly, near the edge of the dirt circle. At the very last second he yells, "LEFT!!!!"

He's wrapped his arms and legs around me in protection and we both come hard into the ground, rolling left. We tumble across the tilled earth, flipping numerous times.

We lie there like lovers, entangled in the lines of a parachute.

Oh. My. God. I don't have any other words other than those in my head.

We sit up.

I am alive. He is alive. We are alive.

The amazing vet, he's taken the brunt of our tumble. We sit there, still attached. He's nicked up all over his arms and bare legs. I think I'm fine, or fine enough. I try out my limbs, look down at my front. I don't believe I have any broken bones.

I look at how far away we are from the rest of the landing parachutes. I want to ask him if I can go again this afternoon. I twist around to see his face. "Can I—"

The amazing veteran, my guy, looks me in the eyes and shakes his head. He tells me he has a whole hell of a lot of paperwork to fill out. We sit staring at the acreage between us, the jump school, and the other jump teams who've landed safely over there, on the near horizon, everyone the size of spiders pulling in their silk webs to use another time. An emergency vehicle from the jump school races across the desert towards us, a huge trailing dust cloud rising behind it.

I was his first primary malfunction. I was also his first secondary chute malfunction. I'm not Irish; I can't blame heritage for my luck.

———

I eventually left L.A. and returned to Toronto, but Joseph and I both were destined for New Orleans. It's an easier place to live, in many ways. We moved back. Joseph stitched together a university gig, four or five adjunct classes a semester, and

I tended bar. I was loathe to teach freshman composition again, especially since I could make more money tending bar four nights a week than I could teaching at a university in New Orleans. It left me plenty of time to work on my novel. I formed Aerial Ink, just women in the trapeze troupe, and stayed massively busy.

My friends have often called me a goofball. I think it's largely accurate. The source of my odd behavior stems from being a firstborn daughter with very moral, non-jokey parents and a perpetual desire to get their attention—a penchant for showing off, born of my gymnastics habit as a kid. Bundle it all together with my love for telling stories, and you've got an odd combo. A goofball.

So the story that earned me a lot of cred at the bar was my When I Jumped Out of a Plane story. The waiters and waitresses loved it. The managers loved it. And the patrons, the ones to whom I might as well have been singing "*Let me entertain you, let me be your guide*," well, they loved it too. I can't say they were enraptured, but they were definitely into the narrative. I used a lot of physical gestures. The veteran jumper jerking at the lines behind me. Here comes the ground—BBBBRRRRRRRRRRRMMMMMMM!!!—barreling up, because that's what it feels like, the ground rising.

Who is this freak of a woman? Who knows. Fun story though for the price of a gin and tonic.

I kept telling people that I'd be good to go, to jump out of planes again, all the rest of my days. I'd already gotten rid of any curse. Primary and secondary malfunction. Boom. Mic drop. The end.

Some of the restaurant/bar staff and I hung out a lot. We gave each other birthday gifts. Several years after my first jump from a plane in California, I received a birthday gift certificate for another parachute jump, this time over the rural flat land of Mississippi, a short drive from New Orleans. I'd get to bring a second person to jump too. Joseph wasn't game. None of the gift-givers were willing. I couldn't comprehend why nobody else wanted to jump out of a plane.

Only one person in my trapeze troupe took me up on it. I couldn't believe all the women wouldn't be clamoring for the opportunity to leap from—this time even higher than my first—12,500 feet! After all, we trapeze women dealt in heights. Our currency. No nets. Come on!

Heather, my trapeze mate, and I drove together out to the Mississippi jump school. Heather, a beautiful and curvy ginger, smart as a whip, was the girlfriend of one of my best friends from graduate school. She could have been as excited as I was to do this thing. For me, once again, to *fly*.

In the car ride, we came up with the plan of letting them, the people we'd be strapped to, know we were aerialists and that we knew our way around being upside down. Maybe they'd actually let us do some spins and flips and stuff. How cool could that be? We can try, right? Let's just mention it and see what we get.

The way I remember it, we don't opt for air conditioning in the car. Or maybe there isn't any. We listen to music on the way to the jump site. I'm going to say The Replacement's "Can't Hardly Wait" is playing, because it suits the scene but also because it's one of my favorite songs ever, and I know Heather likes it.

We park and spring out of the car.

I let Heather know a bit of what to expect. It's both the same and a little different from the Perris site in California.

In Mississippi, the jump site has multiple buildings, one a large, open outbuilding where the trusted humans who belong to the pro jumpers pack their parachutes under the shade of the roofline. Men and women crouch on the concrete slab and carefully fold and gather chutes. They are serious. They don't really look at us clients or pay much attention to anything other than what they are doing. Spiders folding webs in secret, magical patterns. I recognize their actions.

The overseeing professional arranges us in a semi-circle after we've watched the cursory video that says we will never be able to sue. That what we are about to embark on is not their fault. They tell us, in all the legalese, your children will never get any money out of us.

Heather and I don't have children. We sign on the dotted line.

We stand, in the open air, adjacent to the large outbuilding, in mid-morning Mississippi summer heat. The sun bears down. The overseeing professional is going to show us the ropes beyond the videos. He needs a volunteer.

He chooses me although I don't raise my hand.

He needs to demonstrate how we will all be strapped, attached, to another human and how we need to hold our arms and legs. The professional pulls my backside into his front as he demonstrates for the fellow new jumpers how this will go down. And then he just keeps talking and explaining things with his hands on the front of my hips, my butt pulled tight into his groin.

Everybody is paying close attention to what he's telling us. After all, our lives are at stake. The pro is nothing but a pro, but he lets me linger there. I get a little uncomfortable, but close proximity to other people is just a thing. Back when we were clan folk, we probably all piled into a mound to sleep at night in a cave. Get over it, I tell myself. I'm ready to jump out of a plane, and Heather and I are going to tell them we're aerialists and that we are willing and able to spin and flip.

Our group starts prepping for the jump, the altitude as high as legally allowed. We remove jewelry and step into jumpsuits. Texting hasn't yet been invented, but a few people write letters to loved ones to leave in their lockers.

Heather and I get paired up with our people, both guys, mine being the same dude from the demo, and I regale everyone with my first jump story. The word spreads. They quickly nickname me Jinx. "Primary *and* secondary!" they half whisper but then laugh loudly, as if to dismiss any lingering bad juju.

"We're aerialists," Heather volunteers. "We know how to flip in the air. Could we?"

Our guys get a little excited about doing something fun and agree. They show us the sign language shorthand of what we could do, a spinning finger circle this way or that for a left-turning spin or right, a hand flip for forward or backward, a fist for tuck position, flat hand for layouts. This is going to be even better! I'm nutty excited. So is Heather. We grin like halfwits, dressed in our gear as we strap on our helmets and board the plane.

It's sweaty hot in Mississippi for this afternoon jump. From 12,500 feet. That means *more* free fall time. The plane engine starts up. It's loud.

The plane gets going on the ground till yes, here we alight, catching air. They play music in the plane. The jump masters bob their heads, happy to be doing what they're doing. I can't imagine that the adrenaline rush ever goes away completely. A couple of them throw their thumbs at me and yell across the divide things like "Primary and secondary!" and "Jinx!" They think it's dumb funny to tease the head guy about his cargo. If they are nervous to have me among them, they don't show it.

The air is different in Mississippi than in the California desert. The air itself feels heavier, denser. It's certainly more moist. It feels like it will be softer somehow.

I sweat and sweat as we ascend, loop after loop. I practice with my human, my guardian and guide, now securely strapped to my back, with the hand signals, gesturing with my shoulders or body so that he understands that I know how to initiate a back flip or how to spin right. Across the way, I watch Heather do the same.

Some old school rock n' roll plays. Let's pretend it was "Sweet Home Alabama." It would make sense, the Southern bent, albeit one state away.

We're getting up there. Almost there.

And yes, now now!!! Here we go!

The first leap!

The first leap!

Such an extraordinary thought that first human must have had who considered jumping out of a plane. I could go all Icarus, blah blah, but what about the woman who decided she wanted to jump out of a plane and live?

I've always wanted to be a bird. I've always wanted to fly.

I scream in glee.

My guy tests me out first, as I figured he would. Let's try a gentle, slow spin to the right. Ok, good! Let's go left now. Yes!

The ground below us is another canvas, another painting. It's green and more dappled than the desert. It, too, is so beautiful it catches my breath.

Let's try a back layout. Nailed it!

This might well be the singular best time of my life so far. Apologies to past sex partners.

Yes! Let's go for a forward tuck! SWEET!!! Another one! Now two tucks backwards!!

We flip and twist around for well over a minute. I realize at some point how much energy it takes to maneuver against the gravity of free falling—a lot of it at higher speeds than the usual flat-front safe spread. These flips and twists pick up speed. I'm breathing hard from the exertion. The tucks have us going at least 150 miles per hour.

We're descending faster than those who aren't doing tricks, but that's ok. I'm a gleeful cat burglar child gymnast adult trapeze artist in joyous oblivious flight.

My guide and I eventually opt to stop moving so much and enjoy a bit of the scenery. He and I have become separated from the others, by quite a bit.

Some of the others deploy chutes.

Then more.

In Mississippi, the pulling of the ripcord isn't up to me, so I don't have to worry about the essential task.

My guide starts jerking behind me, doing something, but he knows what's what.

Look. Look at that. Everybody else is way over there, and they all have their chutes deployed, drifting slowly in the afternoon sun. How pretty.

My dude, he and I are hurtling towards a highway. Why are we over here, aiming for a highway?

We keep freefalling and freefalling.

This can't be possible. It just can't.

The guy is swearing in my ear. What could he have been thinking? *She's a real jinx. A real one! Jesus Christ in all of Heaven. Why isn't the chute deploying!? I'm pulling and pulling, all my strength, it's not coming, damn it, we're close to 2,500 feet! Fuck. Fuck. Not much time. Come on! What the fuck?!*

We are rushing towards the earth. We are bee-lining to an asphalt highway with cars driving in both directions.

Where is the secondary chute?

Why hasn't he tried that one?

The ground is racing up towards us. Here it comes.

Here comes my last moment.

I love you, Joseph.

I love you, sisters, Dad, Mom.

I don't want to smash like a bug onto a windshield. I don't want to. Somebody help me.

As we get very close to the highway, something happens with the chute. It explodes.

We catch air. Just enough.

And we are down. Right away.

On the ground.

We are ok. We land and crumble hard to our knees and roll, maybe twenty feet from the highway.

The shorn corn stalks are terribly pokey. The low tender greens smell fresh. A cricket thrums out its presence.

In the field, near the highway, we lie and catch our breath. In the far distance, other parachuting people drift down like sparrows.

My guy and I sit up. He can barely breathe as freaked out as he is. We disentangle and dis-attach. He can't believe what has happened.

I'm calm. I am alive. Again.

He claws at our chute. What happened?! He's insanely digging, trying to figure out the source of our near disaster.

The O-rings, or the grommets and pin, some parts of the chute have been packed completely backwards.

He looks as though he might have a heart attack. It's a death sentence, he says. He could have tugged forever, and the chute never would have deployed.

The AAD—the automatic activation device—for our second chute deployed at under 1400 feet, a much lower elevation than it was supposed to. I think about my pro, what his brain could have been clicking through after we'd dropped below 2,000 feet. 1900 feet. *My last jump*, he might have thought. 1800 feet. *Son of a bitch*. 1600. 1500. *Son of a bitch*.

We caught air, barely, just enough, and then were down. That's it. Who knows why it happened. The pro said his wife packed his chutes. Always. He didn't understand. But the AAD worked. Late, but it worked, and we were ok.

Heather and her guy loved their experience. They flipped. They spun. She couldn't have been happier. She didn't land anywhere near the highway.

———

It seems to me—despite how everything is explained—that when I jumped out of planes twice, for the first and second times and had two, no *four* back-to-back colossal parachute malfunctions, that the odds were, are, astronomical. They amount to my winning some ghoulish lottery. *Twice. In a row. The only two times I played.*

Evidently, the odds for the second failure are only the same as the first.

It's hard to wrap my head around.

Regardless, I opted for a Second Chance. I looked that bull straight in the eye, and I took the risk. Gorings can just happen.

I'd do it again.

———

Dad survived pneumonia, and he lived to meet not just another day but a whole other wife after Mom and he split. He and Mary Anne have had decades upon decades of domestic calm. A series of dogs. A lovely existence.

As for Eunice, our babysitter, I still wish I could've known more about her. How did she manage everyday? Maybe her missing hand was a small price to pay for her second chance. Maybe she didn't smile at us girls because she knew we'd never understand her life, her second chance at breathing, at peeling carrots, at standing on a giant ship crossing the Atlantic and peering out at the rolling waves the color of ice in shadow.

Look at her: Eunice, a 22-year-old with one hand. She clutches the ship's railing, the painful nub of her other arm tucked into her coat pocket. She has escaped, while the rest of her family has not. Or here she is, a 22-year-old with two hands, tapping out a drumbeat on the sturdy ship hull, trying to ignore the groans of her empty belly. The doctors will catch the bone cancer in time. She will survive the surgery. Either way. She doesn't know it yet, but she will have a full life and live to be very old. There will be plentiful food, always. There's a second chance coming. And Eunice? She'll take it.

I still have other second chances.

We all do, if we only look.

Junot Diaz published an essay about his adult promiscuity in relation to the sexual abuse he endured as a child before he largely disappeared in the literary world like other men under the sharp gaze of the Me Too movement. I'm certain Joseph believed he'd be next. The Canadian magnifying glass on Joseph had been harsh. It had fried up fellow men like so many ants on the sidewalk.

Post telling me that he'd be having a child with another woman, Joseph had emailed me Junot's essay. I didn't need to read between the lines. I'd lived too long with a person plagued with demons of his own. I'd begged Joseph to take a DNA test for years to determine his heritage. That he should get out in front of it. But it didn't matter. He was going to do what he was going to do. Carve out his own trail.

If I had a second chance to marry or not marry Joseph, which would I choose to repeat?

I don't know.

I honestly don't know.

Shavasana

Balasana
Child's Pose

Child's Pose serves as a shape to sometimes start a practice. We're not supposed to call guided yoga a class, or a routine, or anything other than a practice. I don't usually remember this, but I try. It's taught that we are always practicing, never fully achieving.

A yogi at the front of the room might say, "Let's begin practice in Child's Pose today." More often, though, Child's Pose becomes the suggested retreat pose, the shape where somebody curls into a baby ball on the mat because what's come before has been too exhausting or frustrating or absurdly difficult. It's the 'I Give Up for the Moment' shape, aka a 'restorative pose.' No idea why, but it's always reminded me of a really young puppy just ignoring its new world, plopping its round puppy head into the corner of the pen and pretending to disappear. 'I don't want to play with my litter mates any more,' the pose says. Or for the human it says, 'I don't want to do one more plank. Not even one. Goodbye. I'll be right here, but I can't see you, so you can't see me.' The yoga practice continues all around the practitioner while she or he just hangs out, belly slung low between wide knees. It can be a comforting shape.

In retrospect, whole years passed during our marriage where Joseph and I operated in intermittent Child's Pose. Neither of us wanted to fully address the other one's pain or our shared world that could be immensely difficult. Easier for us to ball up and hide our faces. In the early years of our marriage, we both made grievous mistakes. We had affairs. Plural. But we stayed together somehow or other. We hung in there, didn't leave. We practiced being better at being married. We persevered.

I honestly don't know if either of us should have married, never mind each other. But we did.

We made up our own traditions when they suited us. Poached eggs on rye toast every Sunday morning, WWOZ playing, while we read The New York Times. We had inside jokes that only the other would ever understand, some Kids in The Hall skit imitation or private remembrances, the time the Mississippi River spurted like a geyser through the floorboards of our shack on the wrong side of the levee. What about the time the neighbor brought us over 'very special brownies,' just two in a Ziploc baggy, and neither of us understood how special they were? Joseph said he might need to go on a vision quest after he ate one of the brownies. I ate the second brownie maybe a week afterwards while Joseph was out of town, lay in bed with bad dry mouth, and thought I might have to drive myself to the hospital before I traced back my eating during the past 24 hours. I suddenly couldn't stop laughing, so relieved. I called him and told him I'd figured it all out. I was so stoned! "Remember?" I said, belly laughing. "Remember how you needed to move your table out of the way?!" New peals of laughter from both of us.

Joseph had eaten his brownie for breakfast with coffee on a Saturday. He needed to grade freshman comp papers all day long. He opted to do it on the back deck of the shack, but he thought that the wind had begun a surreal battle with him. He moved his table around the corner, away from the wind, and then back, and back some more till he couldn't back up any farther. How could an entity like the wind be out to get him, on a Saturday morning, while he wrote incoherent comments in the margins of his students' essays? Neither of us ever really smoked weed, so we'd simply not known why the brownies were so special.

Adho mukha savasana
Downward Dog

Downward Dog is intended to become a 'resting pose' if you work on your practice long enough. You get to breathe there for a few counts of inhales and exhales. Yes, your hamstrings work, and your shoulders and back definitely work, but you're supposed to find a bit of respite.

Joseph and I moved around plenty in New Orleans after we returned from Canada. Our first place, the back half of a pretty pale yellow house, had French doors in the bedroom and tall, old windows. I'm not sure how it happened, but I was the one to drive the U-Haul down from Toronto by myself with the two cats and their litter box riding shotgun. Joseph followed in the 4-Runner a week or more later, towing his motorcycle.

For a while, a smart mouse fed itself silly from the inside of the dishwasher in the yellow house. I worried we'd cook it when we ran the dishwasher, but the mouse seemed to know when to get out. And how to get back in. We had a rear yard where Joseph and his friend lifted weights on the scrubby lawn a few days a week. I trained trapeze. I flirted with newly made friends. Joseph did too. Lots. We dressed up in absurd costumes for Mardi Gras and raged away on New Orleans' biggest Tuesday.

After just a year and a half, the owners sold the yellow house in a bidding war in our living room, the one I had painted and decorated to a T, and we had to move quickly. We landed in a smaller apartment, the front portion of a house owned by a friend and fellow teacher. It had a nice side porch. It sat on a busy street. We lived there for five years during a tumultuous span.

For a while, I worked nights, and Joseph days. The morning of September 11th, 2001, Joseph came home early from his usual trip to the coffee shop and told me to get out of bed. He turned on the TV.

Afterwards, I decided to stop messing with other people inside my marriage. I didn't want to do it. The stress, the sneaking around. I'd developed alopecia areata, anxiety-induced, and my hair started falling out in clumps, smooth disks of scalp appearing that I tried to cover up with brushed-over long strands. The brief pleasures of touching a different person simply weren't worth it. I didn't like losing hair, but I really didn't like being a cheater. I wanted to show Joseph how we could both be better people. He could copy me, right? Surely we could move forward together in a healthier way.

Leading by example should have been easier.

You can't hold Downward Dog forever. You stare at your mat between your hands, or just below your face. Often you can look at the people behind you in the same position. That helps.

Others are doing the same thing, holding on, holding on. But eventually fatigue sets in. Your shoulders, carrying so much of the weight, start to ache.

Urdhva mukha savasana
Upward-facing Dog

I don't know where it is anymore, the slip of notebook paper I loved with a crazed passion. I wish I still had it. It never failed to make me smile, more often laugh.

Joseph, well, he wasn't a drawing master, and I guess he'd still admit that. He'd long resorted to all-caps for handwriting. One day I asked him to draw a portrait of the two of us, side-by-side. I want to say it was an eggs and rye toast sort of morning.

He decided to draw us naked in one of his small spiral notebooks. I couldn't tell, at first, if he was actually trying with the drawing or not. I've decided he was drawing caricatures. And that he was also trying his best at that moment.

Joseph drew Naked Joseph as a potato, with a big penis. Joseph drew Naked Amanda as a stick figure with two pancakes for boobs, a tiny bit of bush between her legs. He had them hold hands.

We both busted guts for minutes on end. We came up with nicknames for the potato and the stick, and for years upon years, I used a pushpin in the wall to keep it by my side of the bed. Later, after 9/11, I kept it in my tiny writing space to remind me of what counted.

That I lost the drawing hurts.

Upward dog is never held all that long. It can be a strain on the back. It can be difficult to make sure the chest stays open, the neck relaxed. It's a temporary position, even more so than others.

Virabhadrasana 1
Warrior One

Every single time I take Warrior One, I think about how happy I am for my legs. They hold my weight with elegance. I am ferocious. I am a warrior preparing. I lunge deeper and contract my rib cage, hold my arms aloft, and stare into an imaginary future where I am young again. Or I am old, but I am guiding strong young women who will be fierce for me in the future when I'm no longer able to hold Warrior One with strong legs.

I stare at the wall in front of me, or the person on another mat in front of me, move just my eyes around the room and think, God, we are beautiful in our diversity and ferocity. I love this. I feel human here. I feel like I belong.

Joseph and I still lived in the apartment with the side porch when Katrina hit. We evacuated to Canada for some months. A kind person put a flyer on our car with Louisiana plates for an American Thanksgiving in Toronto. We were welcome to join them for food. I didn't go. I was there alone. Joseph was somewhere or other, as usual, giving a talk or a reading, doing something. Signing books.

I considered beginning a notebook of tally marks for the days Joseph and I spent apart but realized I would have needed to start it years earlier. Maybe one side of the page for days spent together, the other side for days apart. They wouldn't equal out.

Not that much later after we returned to a sad and damaged New Orleans, we moved into another place nicknamed The Compound, a group of five or six apartments on high ground gathered around a large center courtyard. We had friends living there.

Another Mardi Gras arrived. More company arrived. Friends had Snow Queen Bitch staying with them—she was self-named, Canadian, and costumed herself in a white fur Barbarella getup, replete with furry boots. Snow Queen Bitch affixed herself pretty quickly to our houseguest, a Canadian actor who starred in a popular TV show, and she became our houseguest too. Her giggle carried through the thin wall between our bedroom and TV Star's guestroom.

Snow Queen Bitch and TV Star came down with a double case of New Orleans Syndrome, the one where people do things they'd never do anywhere else on earth. The syndrome is so pervasive during Mardi Gras as to be infectious, like psychosomatic flu. Oh, hey, here's an idea, people! Begin the day at 7 AM on Mardi Gras Day, with booze. Pull on your naughty sailor girl costume. Wear the push-up bra. You'll end up losing the peg leg that you made out of super thin plywood by noon today, but for now you like it. It purposely shows some of your butt. Drink something purple from the communal punchbowl on the kitchen counter littered with empty Zapp's potato chip bags and then take some pills. There are ten of you staying in two one-bedroom apartments, and one of them, that guy you thought might be hot at 3 AM, told you that you'd like the pills, so why not? Drink some mushroom tea from the thermos that the woman who's dressed like—a preying mantis, maybe?—is passing around. Pull your best bead strands out of the ridiculous pile resting by the mattress on the floor that your BFF dragged out of her closet for you, the one that's covered in glitter and pieces of two other costumes, the cherry tart pun costume and the mermaid that you hacked off the tail of by 9:30 PM on Bacchcus Sunday because you could only take ten-inch steps, and that just needed to stop because you'd already face-planted half a dozen times.

It's 8 AM, and you all head out. You clatter and clink in your beads, everyone walking pimps with shiny baubles. You imagine yourselves in slow-motion bad-assedness: a preying mantis; a naughty sailor girl; a Spanish moss monster with huge, protuberant, conical monkey tits poking out through the moss with giant red nipples at their ends; a warlock; President Clinton; a topless can-can dancer with flames painted on her breasts; a Slim Jim stick of meat staring through tiny cut-out circles for eyes and wearing an adult diaper inside the conical cardboard costume; a grinning ninny on acid; a young Ruth Bader Ginsberg; and Michael Jackson. You head down St. Charles Avenue to catch Zulu. Maybe a few will get lucky enough to nab a coconut. And then you will walk all the way to the Quarter, or you will first meet up with the Society of St. Anne, a walking parade that anyone can join, and then eventually land in the Quarter later.

Many people don't make it past 3 PM. But many more manage to hang on and party till midnight, when they're literally swept off the streets. The mounted police ride in a phalanx down the road and push people off and into establishments or homes, and the street sweepers come in behind them spraying away mountains of garbage, broken beads, stink, humanity.

I used to dress up for Mardi Gras. I went at it with the best of them. One year when Joseph and I decided to give up booze for Lent, I dressed as the Drink Fairy. I took our biggest suitcase with wheels and loaded it up with all the leftover bottles of alcohol from the past year's parties, stacks of plastic Mardi Gras cups, a couple bags of ice, and wheeled it around behind me, giving people free beverages for miles. I wore a pink dress, a curly blonde wig, wings and glitter. I curtseyed and asked in a falsetto voice if the person I was addressing would like the fairy gift of a free beverage. I opened up the suitcase, and there lay an entire bar.

Joseph, in our earlier days, sometimes seemed to dislike dressing in costume, although I don't think he disliked Mardi Gras in particular. The show was too spectacular. The proximity of strangeness, debauchery, people humping in alleyways and stairwells. Friends, with the freedom of a mask, a costume, turned into the people they'd always dreamt of being, people you didn't recognize at all. I don't think Joseph liked the male gaze on me when I wore something more daring, but at the time I thought, Too Bad So Sad. It was an expression Joseph had taught me. I'd never heard it before I met him. But I definitely liked feeling appreciated.

The Drink Fairy might have marked my last official participation in Mardi Gras. All of it just got old, tired, for me. The crowds, the crowds, the circling for forty-five minutes for parking, the crowds, the sameness of it. I'd grown my way out of dance clubs some years earlier, and now I'd grown my way out of Mardi Gras.

These days I still promise my friends that I will dress one of these years as my self-proclaimed nickname, The Mardi Grinch, and head on down to Bourbon and Jean Lafitte's, but I haven't done it yet.

In inverse proportion, as I began to leave Mardi Gras behind, Joseph grew to love dressing up in costume when he hadn't much before. I suppose my stepping away from the event gave him a measure of freedom he'd not had in the years where I wore a trapeze costume and a wig or striped tights and a short fluffy skirt, drew Raggedy Ann eyes and cheeks on my face and, when asked, told people I was a living doll.

The last years of our marriage, I took the opportunity on Mardi Gras Day to enjoy quiet time at home alone. No chaos, no crowds, no insanity. No houseguests. Just me and Fry. I loved the peace of it. Joseph would don a costume and head out with friends for the entire day and well into the night. Once he dressed as though he were running with the bulls, all white with a red sash, and raced in and out of people as they paraded. Another year he needed to incorporate a wagon because he'd sprained his ankle a couple nights before.

His best costume by far, though, was one that came with a side-kick. One of our closest friends had come over early Mardi Gras morning, and we looted both our closets to come up with a costume for him.

St. Anne is a parade populated almost entirely by hipsters. Dirty hipsters, gay hipsters, rich hipsters, poor. They believe themselves to embody the free spirit attitude of a class-less Mardi Gras, something much different than the original elitist krewes. These days, to ride in a registered parade on a float, and throw beads, costs thousands of dollars per person. St. Anne's is free, and anybody can walk. But it's possible they've now become their own kind of elite. If you are not young enough, or hip enough, or open-minded enough (to what, exactly, morphs from year to year and even block to block) you might simply be ignored. St. Anne paraders are largely white, and they largely wear pastel wigs, gold bodysuits, wings, funky shoes, and anything that sparkles. They are big into puns.

Sons of Anarchy had exploded onto the TV scene the past years. Our friend wore my pink-lavender wig cut in a chin-length bob topped with Joseph's minimal matte black (useless) motorcycle helmet. He wore Joseph's motorcycle jacket, leather chaps, and aviator sunglasses. Our friend became an absurd and brilliant Son of St. Anne-archy.

Joseph? Let's just say he killed it for inventiveness. Our sister-in-law had gifted us at Christmas with an old-school snowshoe fitted with a mirror in its center (to be hung on the wall.) Joseph carried it all the way into the Quarter and back, everywhere he went that day, as his prop. He wore one of my really good, long brown wigs, a real beaver pelt hat with earflaps, a T shirt with an illustration of a deer head in the middle of it, a heavy wool red and black plaid short overcoat tied with a sash, boots, beaded moosehide gloves with fringe, and half of a real moose jaw that hung from a leather cord around his neck for the length of his torso to his groin. He'd stop in the middle of a crowd on Bourbon, halt the pedestrian traffic around him, and gaze lovingly at himself in the mirror.

Everyone is crazy on Mardi Gras Day, so most people just bypassed and kept walking. But plenty of people stopped and stared at Joseph staring at himself. Who is this guy? What is he doing? What *is* he?

He'd pause, blow himself a kiss in the mirror, pet his long hair or sweep it over his shoulder, and turn to the strangers, grinning.

He was The Narcissistic Trapper.

He thought himself immensely funny. I can't imagine that he would dress up as a parody of his true self, but maybe he would. Was that the whole schtichk that made him play the role all day long, up and down Bourbon, Frenchman, and beyond? Maybe he saw through the façade of the invention of The Great Joseph Boyden. Or did he believe himself to be anything but the ruse even though he let it happen? Did he believe himself to be a lowly, humble, down-to-earth guy everybody loved and hence nothing close to a narcissistic trapper? Retrospect offers up nothing to me but irony.

TV Star, a year or two earlier, almost missed his flight on Ash Wednesday. A truck full of something like molasses or rubber cement had capsized on the main highway and stalled traffic to a complete standstill. I decided I simply couldn't swallow more debauchery for yet another day should he not manage to make it to his plane. I was going to get TV Star to the airport. I always drove, in part because should Joseph have had some major infraction, it could have affected his chances for gaining his citizenship easily.

So I drove down the highway shoulder, up, down, and over grass, and onto an off-ramp. I sped through side streets and access roads. And I got TV Star to the airport. He made his flight. I felt like a badass. I felt like a warrior. And I felt very much done with Mardi Gras.

Virabhadrasana 2
Warrior Two

Warrior Two is my favorite warrior. I pretend I'm fencing, or holding a saber. I love making the shape with a strong jaw, proud neck, an unblinking stare, and trying to take it as deep as I'm able. In the past year that I've practiced yoga six or seven days a week, I've likely spent hours total in Warrior Two. It is my angriest pose. It is my Do You Think I'd Roll Over and Die? pose.

I've hated confrontation since I was a child. I hate fighting, arguing, screaming and yelling. It quite literally nauseates me. If I'm at odds with a person close to me, I fail to eat, sometimes for an entire day. After having spent 25 years with Joseph, he'd learned my inclinations down to the minutia, and something he figured out was that I was loathe to initiate a fight or ask him about behavior I found not just inappropriate but wrong. I believe I must have come across as a bit of a chicken, considering how many times these last two plus years people have asked, "Surely you knew?" or "You guys had an open marriage, right?"

It's impossible for me to know what Joseph told other people, but no, I never agreed to an open marriage.

And yes, I think, in the darkest recesses of my addled brain, I knew things were still not right with my marriage despite my having stepped up to an honorable place. Hidden phone records, pharmacy receipts he forgot to throw away. It.

She. Them. Hiding in a figurative dishwasher like a mouse. Or under my nose at public events, as brazen as a cougar standing on a garage roof in broad daylight. How exciting that must have been for them to press so close to each other in a crowd with me mere feet away. How dangerous. What a thrill.

My next Warrior Two, I'm taking it so deep I'll be in the splits. But with my front knee still aloft. It will be my best Warrior Two I've ever done yet. Because I have hours more to do before my final resting pose.

Virabhadrasana 3

Warrior Three

I despise Warrior Three. I am not balanced. I am not a good teeter-totter. My hypermobility syndrome helps not in the least; my knee joints won't stabilize. Muscling through the pose is my only option.

If I were allowed to turn out my standing foot and raise the elevated leg in a turned-out position too, hold my arms in something like airplane arms, but more graceful, I could do it just fine. I'm willing to bet I could even do it on a balance beam.

But I can't do that. There are ways that shapes should be done in yoga.

After all, it's not a dance. At least in an organized practice, your shapes should be like the others'. You can't just go out there and do whatever the hell you feel like.

Because it's wrong to say to your wife, "I've decided to just live my own life," and not explain what shape that's actually going to take.

Vrschikasana

Scorpion

In May, 2015, Joseph and I planned for two major events and booked our travel back-to-back. On my side of the family, our niece would be graduating from high school, and my sister Meg and Lance were throwing a huge party. On his side of the family, our nephew was getting married at a destination wedding in Mexico, on a postcard beach with blue, blue waters. We'd first fly out to Nebraska and then a few days later head south of the border for the wedding.

The night before we were to fly out to Nebraska, Joseph and I had a massive, screaming, yelling, horrible-horrible fight, something I was just about incapable of doing. But pushed into a corner long enough, poked with a stick like a wild animal in a cage, I let loose, and we fought into the wee hours.

After I could no longer engage, I went to lie on the sofa in our living room but never really slept, opened my eyes with first light and collected my thoughts. We'd been so angry at one another. Could we make this trip work with all the vicious fighting? We didn't have much of a choice.

I've never done well when sleep-deprived. My brain feels loose in my skull, my eyes don't want to coordinate, and I feel far worse than any hangover. My body tells me in no uncertain terms that it needs more sleep. I didn't have the option though.

We made it to the New Orleans airport, neither of us willing to take up where we'd left off, checked luggage, and waited for our first flight. We were connecting in Houston.

Food options weren't great at the old MSY airport, so I opted for a fresh fruit bowl and some sausage patties that weren't swimming in grease.

On the plane, I couldn't keep my eyes open. As the other passengers boarded, my neck would slowly bend backwards, and I'd choke myself awake, my face aimed straight at the plane's ceiling.

"I really need some sleep," I told Joseph, and he took pity on me. Still flexible, I contorted myself into a position that allowed me to stay buckled into my seatbelt while I lay my head on Joseph's thigh as a makeshift pillow.

It's a short flight, New Orleans to Houston, but I slept. Probably just not long enough.

When we deplaned, Joseph said he wanted to get a shoeshine. "Really?" I asked. "Please, let's just go to our next gate." My neck had gotten stuck, kinked almost, in a crooked position from sleeping so twisted up on the plane. I was lightheaded, a little dizzy. "Please don't," I said. "I feel really funny."

Joseph wanted a shoeshine though, so he stepped up into a shoeshine chair and set his carry-on next to him on the floor. I couldn't convince him otherwise.

"I'm going to the bathroom then," I told him, and walked towards one of the major intersections of the terminal where five or six hallways converged like spokes into the hub of a wagon wheel.

I stopped in the middle of the hub and looked around. I lost my footing slightly, my heavy laptop satchel and purse both on my right shoulder. I was decidedly dizzy. I looked for signs for the women's room. Up in the rafters, two sparrows chirped. I lifted my head to look at them, and they dove, flying straight towards me. I followed their quick flight, throwing my head back at an angle to watch them careen over me. I had one nanosecond of awareness before everything went black. I thought, "Oh, well this isn't up to me anymore."

According to one of the witnesses, I fell like a cut-down tree in the woods. I smashed onto the concrete floor of the Houston Airport, and—whether my head cracking onto concrete caused it or I had already entered into it with the jerk of my head towards the birds—I had a grand mal seizure.

The witness had noted that Joseph and I had come in together, and she had the sense to seek him out in his shoeshine chair. She told him something was wrong with me.

Joseph later said that he thought I was dying. I convulsed in the middle of hundreds of people, flopping like a fish on the floor, everyone stopping to stare. Joseph had no idea what to do. Biting my tongue, I foamed blood at the mouth. My convulsions went on and on for minutes on end.

At some point a doctor appeared, an East Indian man who crouched near Joseph and me. He checked my vitals and said he didn't believe I was breathing. He turned me onto my side. I continued to jerk and flop.

During emergencies, time slows. It's hard to say how long I remained in the grand mal, in the big bad. No other airport emergency help appeared for well over ten minutes, closer to twenty, if Joseph is to be believed. Other airport staff though thought it a good idea to form a circle around Joseph, the doctor, and me. Joseph said they all faced outwards and tried to get passersby to move on, to not stop and stare at the flopping woman foaming blood out of her mouth on the concrete floor. Joseph seemed to find the workers' behavior admirable.

I came to on the gurney. Finally.

We rode in an ambulance to the hospital. I was checked out and given a number of tests. Joseph made arrangements for our luggage to be sent back to New Orleans, and we returned home the next day.

Forced to contemplate my life once again, I admit to having been quiet. To having been scared beyond almost all measures. I was alive, once more, but who knew what was wrong with me?

A grand mal seizure in the middle of an airport isn't a small deal. Numerous times Joseph repeated that he thought I was dying. I had additional MRIs and CATs to schedule, a brain specialist to see. Would I have another seizure in a day or a week or a month? Seizures can often be the harbingers of brain cancer. I understood that a grand mal seizure out of nowhere wasn't a fortuitous event.

We missed our niece's graduation party. I tried not to alarm my side of the family. I wanted to keep the celebration going. But I had to tell everyone why I wouldn't make it.

Maybe 24-48 hours after Houston, Joseph hatched his own plan. He'd fly my mom to New Orleans to look after me, and he would continue on to the destination wedding, in Cancun, with his swim trunks, to the prepaid hotel room. After all, Joseph's firstborn son shouldn't have it all to himself, right?

Joseph had started a habit of 'asking' me if I was ok with him going somewhere, doing something, when it was merely a formality. He was going to do what he was going to do. He was just going to live his life, the way he saw fit, the way he wanted to. He told me that. I should have fully understood what that meant.

And he wanted to go swim in blue, blue waters and forget about his flopping fish of a wife.

So that's what he did.

His decision to leave me, then, told me I no longer mattered enough to deserve his time and care. I should have seen the handwriting, in all caps, on the wall. Handwriting experts say people who write in all caps have a lot to hide.

Six months later, Joseph figured out a way to go to Europe with baby mama. Hey, he had a chance to go live in France and write for free! As a writer-in-residence. He stuck his hand in the puppet Amanda and made a ridiculous show of it, making sure *I'd* be the one to say how difficult the trip would be for me, gone for weeks and weeks while the dog was back in New Orleans without me. He knew I wouldn't go. He got his wish.

In the following two years, he figured out that it was easier to greet the dog first at the door when he returned home from one trip or another, averting his gaze from me entirely. He'd say, "Hello! Hello, Fry! Hello, buddy!" and shower Fry with affection as I stood there with my hand on the doorknob.

"Hello, Amanda," I'd finally say, not moving out of the open door, forcing him to finally lift his face towards mine. He looked sour. It was an expression I never fully understood, as though he had a bad taste in his mouth.

Now I know, in hindsight, what the bile of guilt looks like.

Scorpion Pose is an advanced shape. It requires strength, balance, and flexibility in equal measures. When I need to corral all my residual anger, all my frustration at the lost years, when I want to feel like I could sting someone, I kick up into Scorpion. Let me show you how much I will not be hurt ever again. Let me show you how I will defend myself from splintering apart. Let me show you my reserves of fortitude. Let me show you how you cannot kill me. I am a writer who often worked in anonymous service to you, but I will wait in your shoe, and you will remember, always, to check where you place your feet. I won't be stepped on, ever, ever again.

Of course these are just words from a pained human being. And it's evidently the smallest, the youngest scorpions who have the strongest poison. I'm certainly not that anymore, but that doesn't matter. I've decided: screw the expression of 'physician heal thyself' or whatever it is. It's better another way. Writer: heal thyself.

Get better. It's time.

Svarga Dvidasana
Bird of Paradise

I believe in grace as both a concept in multiple religions as well as a tool to use moving through the real world in real time. I aspire to be graceful. These days I aspire to bring a measure of grace to the dissolution of my marriage.

Bird of Paradise is often seen as another immensely difficult pose. Stand on one leg, bind the other with your entwined arms, and stand, holding your other leg, aloft, over your head.

A lot of the names of yoga poses don't make much visual sense to me. Crow Pose doesn't really look like a crow anyway I can construe it. Rabbit? It looks like a stone. So it makes me happy to see a Bird of Paradise in the actual pose, all spiked elegance and bravado. It's beautiful, and I aim to approximate the namesake.

I want to remember my marriage as not all lost time, and I think I can do that now. Surely Joseph couldn't have been so miserable with me as to just use me for my editing, my writing support, for my making a nice home for him to spend time in occasionally and that's just it. That's a wrap.

Strangely, searching for moments of grace with Joseph still doesn't come easily. Part of my memory failure, I think, is that we ultimately spent so little time alone with just one another. My husband grew up as one of a wolf pack, and he found comfort in the company of *many* others. I grew up an introvert, and to spend my time constantly with an ever-changing crew wasn't easy, but Joseph preferred it. He went to coffee shops to write. I hid myself in a cubbyhole at home. If we ever took a working vacation, Joseph almost immediately attached himself to others at the event. Sherman Alexie in Australia, Junot Diaz in Jamaica.

One of our trips to Paris, Joseph wanted to go to the top of the Eifel Tower. As many times as I'd been to the city, I'd never been to the top—I guess wrongly thinking the gesture gauche. But we went up, one night while one or both of us were there on book tour, and landed up top just about midnight. He and I had never had a honeymoon for poverty reasons more than anything else. After a few years, when we had a bit of money, we kept coming up with ideas for a getaway, but they never materialized. So this would be a romantic and momentous, if short, experience.

And then, right then on top of the Eifel Tower, there was Joseph's student from UNO in New Orleans. At midnight. On top of the Eifel Tower. Our possible moment, his and mine, melted away into a good half hour with the student and her friend.

In my memory, it's how it almost always went.

I think our best times were spent across from each other at a messy paper-strewn table. We wrote and wrote. We read sentences and paragraphs and pages to each other. We reread. We made suggestions. We interrupted but then waited for the other to catch up, find a word, complete a phrase, search for something.

Grace hovered over that table.

Sometimes Grace bounced around our whole library. Damn, we had a *library*.

Grace. She wants me to say something: if you need to blame me, you can. It's my gift.

I hunch my crouching body with my twisted arms wrapped around a kinked leg. I stare at the ground.

It's time to rise.

I unfurl, and I stand on a single wobbly leg till it sturdies.

I. Am.

Shavasana

Corpse Pose

There are eight limbs of yoga. Only one involves making shapes with the physical body.

In Kansas City, in the depths of my journey to nowhere I yet understood, I took a yoga workshop on another limb of yoga practice and learned about *Ahimsa*. It translates, most literally, as 'not to injure' and 'compassion.' It's "inspired by the premise that all living beings have the spark of the divine spiritual energy, therefore, to hurt another is to hurt oneself."

Neither Joseph nor I practiced *Ahimsa* towards one another. We should have, but we didn't. It's hard.

Now, though, I can at least practice forgiveness. I have to. To be able to rise up in Bird of Paradise, or arch over in Scorpion, I have to forgive. It's all I've got.

In my recent practice led by a young woman with an old soul, she talked some about the theme of the month for December, the elements: water, air, earth, fire.

She concentrated our practice on fire that day and led us through an hour and a half of twisting poses and inversions. At the end she said, as we melted our way into Corpse Pose, that the fire we held could now be extinguished. The fire goes out. It is extinguished. It's funereal. Shavasana is a burning away of the body to ash.

Let go, she said. Let go.

And so I did.

What did Virgil the crow think when Joseph captured him, wrapped him up in a hoodie, held him tight against his chest, and rode him on a bike down busy city streets? Pain, maybe, or just fear.

Despite our limited resources, we bought a large cage for Virgil and parked it right behind me in my narrow writing hallway. When we saw Virgil had become bored and wasn't going to ever tuck his wing back into his side neatly like the other, we read up on what we could do. We made cloth strips to tie in knots on his multiple perches for him to untie. Crows like puzzles. We learned his favorite food—something a little cannibalistic—was fried chicken bones. Eventually his social nature kicked in. Crows need their others around them, and Virgil had none. Sometimes in the morning or the middle of the afternoon, hearing other crows cawing outside, he called out past his cage into the void. It broke my heart.

Virgil started plucking off his lower feathers, bit by bit. He finally looked like he wore no pants, his plump pink thighs ending in his skinny black shins and huge taloned black feet. I couldn't bear it.

We found a bird sanctuary to take Virgil in, and Joseph and Virgil made the drive across the lake without me. The sanctuary volunteers said that they would amputate the long dislocated wing and place Virgil with another one-winged, non-flying crow in a large, secure enclosure. They would bond, the people promised.

It's what Joseph told me. And it's what I believed.

Epilogue

In mid-January 2020, I drove from New Orleans to St. Louis on a mission to move my mother from St. Louis to just outside Omaha. Mom's Alzheimer's had grown worse, and she couldn't live without more daily care. Meg would be able to visit Mom every day in a senior facility that would allow Mom to keep her autonomy and her cat Lucy for a while longer.

Mom knew, or pretended to forget, that she'd be moving away from St. Louis. She'd written it on her calendar attached to the side of her refrigerator with magnet clips. I'd spent Christmas with her just three weeks previous. But when I arrived back in St. Louis again, Mom had done next to nothing in the way of packing.

Christmas had proven disastrous. Meg and her family were supposed to drive from Nebraska to St. Louis. Emily and family had booked a holiday skiing trip in Colorado months previous. So I flew up to keep company with Mom and Dad, some 40 years divorced. Dad's wife Mary Anne had recently needed to be moved out of their house and into a care facility. The weather didn't cooperate for the Nebraska contingency though, and all plans fell through. Christmas would be Mom, Dad, and me. Just like my first three years of life.

Dad came over for Christmas Eve dinner, and he would reappear for a Christmas Day mid-day meal after he returned from his church. Christmas Eve we had crab legs and lobster tails and everything else I could attempt as fancy and celebratory despite the circumstances. Mom had baked cookies for dessert.

Christmas Day, a few hours before Dad was supposed to come over again, he called me. Mary Anne had collapsed at the nursing home, and those on staff believed she'd died. She had not, but she'd been shuttled off to the ER, and Mom and I were left to eat alone. Dad would spend his Christmas Day in the hospital, waiting for word on Mary Anne.

A few days after Christmas, Mary Anne had recovered, and I had to go with Mom to donate her car to her church. She didn't understand why we'd needed to do it. Every time I visited, her car seemed to sport multiplying dings and dents, but I might have been imagining things. That wasn't the reason. I explained to Mom repeatedly that she wouldn't need a car in Nebraska. Meg would take her shopping or on errands. I'd stopped trying to get Mom to admit she had Alzheimer's. The few times I tried, very gently in a non-confrontational way, she clenched her jaw and set her face in a version of I will never say that word and screw you for saying that to me because I gave birth to you and you have no right. Then Mom would turn her face away from mine. So I started saying simpler things like she didn't need her car anymore. When that didn't work, I tried to remind her that she'd been mandated to retake both her written and driving tests again and that she had missed the deadline—the truth.

Each day, sometimes many times a day, the same questions came. Why couldn't she drive anymore? Why was she moving to Nebraska?

Mom didn't remember that she had a memory care doctor.

After hours of searching through desk drawers and file cabinets, we'd miraculously found her car title. I showed her, and told her, I had the paperwork to bring to the church in my purse. I didn't know where Mom's church was, so I said I'd follow her there in my car. She turned onto a four-lane major thoroughfare, and I turned after her. Maybe half a mile down the busy street, Mom came to a dead stop in the right-hand lane, threw open her door, and walked towards me, her car door hanging open into the left-hand lane.

I unrolled my window as I panicked, glancing in my rearview. "What are you doing?!" I hollered at her.

"Where are the papers?" she asked.

"What, Mom?!"

"The papers for the car!" she screamed, standing in the road.

In the New Year, Fry and I flew back to New Orleans, and my small personal world rematerialized.

Dear April and I went to watch the heartbreaking Saints playoff game January 2nd. The bar swarmed with visiting Australians, a dozen TVs slung from the ceiling. A day and a half later, on April's birthday, we were both feeling the beginnings of a cold. We opted for pho as a lunchtime panacea and then parted.

A few days later, we both ended up monster sick. I hadn't been sick in over three years, so I'd nearly forgotten what it felt like. April might have felt even worse, if that's possible. Who knows what we had. We were sick for two weeks, but I needed to be well. I needed to drive to St. Louis and pack up Mom and get her to Nebraska.

As soon as I wasn't hacking up lungs, I headed north once again with Fry in my car. I called Mom multiple times from the road to remind her I was on my way.

—————

Emily had sorted Mom's closets for days and donated multiple bags of clothes and blankets to charities—sneezing all the while with her cat allergy—but Mom hadn't packed anything at all. I worried I wouldn't be able to pull off the move.

I boxed and wrapped and sorted and culled ten or more hours a day. I took one morning off to go with Dad to the nursing home where Mary Anne had landed. She no longer wanted to eat much. We sat with her in a pretty dining room, and Dad ate her delicious filet of sole. The drive to the facility, however, was long for our father, and tedious. He asked if maybe I could visit another closer facility to see if it made sense for Mary Anne. I went with Dad again the next day and told him I thought the closer place was picture perfect.

In those ten days of packing before the Pod would arrive, I lost my patience with Mom. I grew fatigued with the physicality of the task, the repeated questions, the pulling-teeth discussion we had every half hour about why she couldn't take everything, how she'd be downsizing, that she would only be taking the nicest and best of her belongings. The sometimes egregious displays of Mom's obstinacy wore me down. When the day finally came that Mom understood she'd really be moving out of her favorite house, she made a show of her anger, something I'd never seen before. She kicked apart a birdbath. She grabbed dishes out of her kitchen and busted them on her back sidewalk. I asked her what she was doing, *why* was she doing that, and she replied, "What does it matter? It's all garbage anyway."

Emily, family, and I loaded up the Pod in the brutal freezing cold. The Pod got taken away. And Mom and I, and Fry and the cat Lucy, headed up the cobbled lane to Nebraska.

Lucy had never been in a car. She cried the whole way in her carrying case, for eight hours. Fry sat on my lap in the driver's seat, his ears pinned back for the pain of Lucy's howls.

I am so sorry, Mom. I am so, so sorry I had to make you go.

Meg now carries the burden of helping Mom before she's moved again into a memory care or nursing care facility. Meg is a special human. She will take on the weight of this and then some. She understands the nature of transience.

I stayed a few days longer in Nebraska than I needed to after we'd gotten Mom safely into her new apartment, the Pod unloaded, the familiar furniture into her new third story place, the clothes in the closet. I thought that I'd make the long drive back with Fry to St. Louis to watch the Super Bowl there, but Lance caught me off guard and made me cry for his kindness. He could see how exhausted I was. He offered to have me stay at their house in their slice of heaven, the place where Fry and their sweet pit bull Rainie both shared a dog bed in front of the fireplace, till the Monday after the game.

At least the long and tiring drive back to St. Louis wasn't treacherous, the roads dry. I would stay at Dad's, since Mom's house was empty of furniture and Emily's full of her family.

Dad and Mary Anne had kept separate bedrooms for some years. I would sleep in Mary Anne's vacant lavender bedroom and try not to wake Dad with his early bedtime and my late night habits.

The next day, the phone rang at 5:30 in the morning.

I knew before I heard Dad scrambling to reach the phone in his study.

I drove Dad to the nursing home where Mary Anne had passed in the night. Gracious and giving people had covered her with her favorite cashmere throw on top of the covers. Someone had brushed her hair and put a bit of lipstick on her mouth. I could only think about how peaceful she looked. She was so truly at peace.

I waited out in the lobby while Dad spent his last minutes with Mary Anne's body. A nurse pushed a cart past me as I cried in the middle of their day, the other inhabitants being delivered their breakfasts in the dining room. A man called out to the world from down the hall, over and over, "Help! Help me! Somebody help me!"

I asked the passing nurse if he yelled like that all the time. The woman told me that yes, as long as he was awake he did, but that he was as cared for as he could possibly be. Then she told me that I looked like I needed a hug. I stood and accepted her gift, the extraordinary gift of an embrace from a complete stranger.

And then she pushed her cart down the hall.

I helped Dad with arrangements. For over a week, I slept in Mary Anne's bed every night. I made food Dad couldn't eat for a lack of appetite. But he held it together, his pastor a pillar of strength.

Now. Here and now in the middle of a pandemic, I think about all that touching. The hug from the nurse. Shaking the funeral director's hand, embracing Mary Anne's family members who'd made the journey to her memorial. I think often about small measures of physical kindness.

I think because I am still so alone, the notion of touching another human being tugs at me in a way that maybe Jimmy Fallon with his crawling kids on his filmed-from-home show doesn't. The yearning for tactile comfort is something real.

And I suspect it's something that the elderly and alone crave. The ones who don't have grandkids clasping their legs, the ones who can't go to the senior rec centers anymore. Or bingo. Or their Tuesday chess game or bridge match.

For whatever reason, I've had *Jumanji* dreams for years—like the old school Robin Williams *Jumanji*. I dream that I can still leap and jump like I did as a kid, and I am a guide for others who aren't quite as agile as I am. I can sidestep bears swinging their clawed paws at me and out-leap cougars. When I was still married, I used to have my *Jumanji* dreams and be the leader of Joseph and me. I'd show him where we'd need to jump from one building to another. Follow me! I'd yell at him in my dream. Come this way!

Last week I had another one of the dreams, and this one had me packed into a large populated bedroom, as though I had a family, a couple kids and a partner. Along with nutria and snakes, a juvenile alligator roamed the room that I kept trying to guide my imaginary family away from. I'd jump on top of the bed, bounce up to the light fixture and grab it, and tell the kids to stay off the floor. The alligator was on the floor. And then a kitten appeared. I said out loud in my dream to everybody who refused to listen to me, "Oh, great, and now there's a kitten."

When I trained gymnastics six days a week as a young girl, the coach of our elite team decided that after three hours of training every weeknight we needed to run cross country. Around and around he had us run through the huge facility, up and down staircases, down the long hallways, around the exterior of the ice hockey rink, the basketball court. We ran barefoot, in our leotards, a line of tiny, muscled, flat-chested girls. In that year's physical fitness test at school, I crushed the half-mile. Hell, I got to wear shoes outside.

There will be more moments again, I think. Groups of girls and boys doing things together. And there will be greater appreciation for those moments. Not one of the girls or boys in home quarantine will forget these days.

April's daughter and son will remember. All of Gord's kids, Emily's, Meg's. And they will make something of their future opportunities. They will build a better world. Maybe another generation will run circles around us and fix this mess we've left them. Maybe the imaginary daughter I never adopted will make a fist and decide that the earth is worth fighting for. She'll know to avoid the alligators. Maybe she will find a mushroom growing in a forest that cures cancer.

She, too, will believe in the leap.

Pink Dogwood Song

Against a dark sky, pink blooms.
Petals raised, beggars, believers
At prayer, praise, awake, at home

Safe by my window, alive
To a moment of sun before
The north cloud's rising. I have

Watched my one die, she dearer
Than life to me. Little choir, come
In me, teach me to flower.

—*Bill Buege, my father, April 2020*

Acknowledgements

Fiction is my first genre, my first child. The truthful words on these pages didn't always come easily. If it weren't for the encouragement and support of many, I would have crumbled and given up. One special person over these last years perpetually had my back. For days and weeks and endless months, she checked in on me, taking on my pain as her own and replacing it with love. Dear sister Meg, I could never have gotten up that mountain without you. I know you saw the easier coming descent for me when I could not.

Dad, you have inspired me my entire life. Thank you for the gift of your luminous poetry and steady guidance. Mom, your gentle heart is magical. I couldn't have asked for better parents or a childhood more filled with wonder. Emily, sweet baby sister Emily, you've grown into a fierce, beautiful, wickedly smart warrior. I love you all.

Other family has remained stoically supportive in my fight to claw my way up. Lance, I'd trust you with my life all over again tomorrow—on your shoulders on top of a ladder three stories up. Cheri, Lore, and cousins, I feel your kindness across the miles. Karen, you too will rise. I know it. Nieces and nephews, you've brought me unbridled joy over the years. Your futures are wide open. Go. Fly.

Rudy and Barb, you both are often in my thoughts. I wish you continued strength.

Far-flung others, your friendship is palpable, your texts, emails, and messages so welcomed and valued: Jeni and Daniel, Nick, Bill G., Tanya T., April Y-R. and Migizi, Karma Tribe goddesses, Tim F., Christine H. (mover extraordinaire), Jim and Diane. Laura Boyden and Susan Boyden, thank you for never abandoning me.

Still more, closer to home, keep me company and keep me sane: Marc B., Kelcy and Lucy, Jenny and Dave, Meredith and Jesse, Jodi, Shamicka, Jared Z., Frank B., and all the talented teachers at Wild Lotus.

AC, Philip, Erin, Cate, Joe V., Les W., I am so thankful for your time and keen eyes and ears. You offered me invaluable feedback and notes. Creighton, you were the first to read the earliest full draft. Thank you. I promise to return the favor.

Miles, rarest of INFJs, someday I hope you know in your heart that you, too, saved me from the flood.

Melissa, you gave me beautiful shelter and a shoulder to cry on. Nanc, how many years have you given me the same? Next Easter, damn it, we'll share a feast. Shari, kindest Shari, Kansas City would have been a wasteland without you. Thank you for your generosity of heart and time. And April? You brilliant, resolute spitfire, you. Next time I will give you the clothes off my back.

When we were still married, Joseph bought me a funny T shirt, a play on *Game of Thrones*. In the series' iconic lettering, the T says *Mother of Chihuahas*. I still wear it happily. People in the grocery store—the ones who know the show—always smile or laugh. Like Daenerys, I've had a trio of fire-breathers fighting for me. Honor Molloy, Kevin Fortuna, and Bill Lavender, when I could no longer climb, you carried me over the peak. You really, truly did.

———

For anyone interested in my sister's special abilities, she can be found here: readingsbymeg.com

Lavender Ink
New Orleans
lavenderink.org

CPSIA information can be obtained
at www.ICGtesting.com
Printed in the USA
LVHW091720101220
673844LV00005B/148